N**O** B.S.

PRICE STRATEGY

THE ULTIMATE NO HOLDS BARRED

KICK BUTT

TAKE NO PRISONERS

GUIDE TO PROFITS, POWER, AND PROSPERITY

Dan S. Kennedy & Jason Marrs

EP
Entrepreneur.
Press

Publisher: Jere L. Calmes
Cover Design: Andrew Welyczko
Production and Composition: Eliot House Productions

This publication is designed to provide accurate and authoritative information in regard to the subject matter covered. It is sold with the understanding that the publisher is not engaged in rendering legal, accounting or other professional services. If legal advice or other expert assistance is required, the services of a competent professional person should be sought.

Library of Congress Cataloging-in-Publication Data
Kennedy, Dan S., 1954–
    No B.S. price strategy/by Dan Kennedy and Jason Marrs.
        p.   cm.
    ISBN-10: 1-59918-400-1 (alk. paper)
    ISBN-13: 978-1-59918-400-5 (alk. paper)
        1. Pricing. I. Marrs, Jason. II. Title.
    HF5416.5.K46 2010
    658.8'16—dc22   2010033556

Printed in the United States of America

15 14 13 12   10 9 8 7 6 5 4 3 2 1

Contents

SECTION II
SAMPLES

SECTION III
RESOURCES

Price, Profit, Power, and Prosperity

(Why and How This One Book Can Be Worth at Least One Million Dollars to You)

Dan Kennedy

Price bedevils.
It lurks in the bushes, waiting until the sale is almost made, to leap out and scream "Boo!" Retailers fear Walmart, to such extent some close their businesses at the mere announcement that Walmart is coming to town. The real source of their terror is price. Grown, mature adults engaged in B-to-B sales quake in their boots at the prospect of facing a purchasing agent who is known to drive a hard bargain. Business owners routinely under-price their goods and services to come in below competitors, surrendering to the fear of losing customers by being judged unreasonably expensive—oddly unaffected by the more appropriate fears of losing profits in the short-term, losing their business to bankruptcy in the long-term. (Few lowest-price providers have ever avoided this fate.) Price is a terrorist.

In the 1930s and 1940s, Walter Gibson, writing as Maxwell Grant, churned out hundreds of pulp novels featuring the mysterious crime-fighter, "The Shadow." There was also a radio show, and more recently, a failed movie starring Alec Baldwin. The Shadow struck such fear in evil-doers that, often, only his eerie laugh was necessary for their surrender. Living in fear that The Shadow would suddenly emerge from the dark with cape swirling and guns blazing, they were terrorized by *all* shadows, virtually driven insane by fear.

Like The Shadow, price strikes fear in the hearts of salespeople and business owners alike—to such extent it compels business owners to reduce their prices without any real marketplace pressure to do so or testing to validate their fear-based decisions. To such extent it makes the salesperson's voice quiver and palms sweat and body language go sour when he arrives at presentation of price, telegraphing to his prospect that the price is too high. Like the evil-doers terrorized by all shadows, business owners are terrorized by their fears about price rather than by any reality.

Fear is a powerful thing. Another comic hero, Batman, is brought to his knees by the super-villain, The Scarecrow, his only weapon is a magic dust that creates unbridled horrific imaginings of each person's worst fears. Sprayed in one person's eyes it instantly triggers that individual's worst, secret nightmares. Sprayed over an entire city, it produces mass-hypnosis, filling the streets with imaginary monsters assaulting the population, sending each person into spiraling horror they will do anything to escape—including killing others and themselves. The Scarecrow is a brilliant comic book creation, because he has no real power. His only power comes from the fear he can create in others, a turnabout of the idea behind his hero enemy Batman, who chose his bat identity and costume and mystery to "strike fear in the hearts and minds of evil-doers."

In business, fear-based decisions turn out badly; fear-driven behavior weakens and ultimately destroys. I personally watched the owner of a thriving $100-million-a-year company give over a significant share of profits and control of his operations to a bullying, mostly bluffing competitor who threatened to destroy the business with lower prices and massive advertising if he wasn't brought in as a partner. Once a partner, this "terrorist" destroyed the business from within in order to create a vacuum in the market rather than compete head-on. I and many others cautioned the company owner against voluntary capitulation rather than battle with possibilities of victory or at least defeat with honor. There were reasons to believe the well-capitalized and ruthless bully seeking entry to and instant dominance of this market could be turned back. It didn't require simple blind faith or stubborn determination to triumph against a well-capitalized and aggressive but naïve and historically inept challenger. Still, this company owner was vanquished not by that opponent, but by his own fear of that opponent.

Not to say that paranoia is forbidden. Former CEO of the once-giant corporation ITT, Harold Geneen, while leading its rescue, said "Only the paranoid survive." No business owner can skip, prance, and dance along whistling a happy tune, drunk with his own optimism, in denial of all risks, hazards, threats, and problems; nor, specific to price, can he merely do as he pleases, as whim inspires, with no regard for his customers' abilities and willingness to pay or for competitive factors. A sense that the ground beneath is truly ice, and vigilance about thin spots, is required of anyone running a business or his own sales career. One of my pet principles is that, whatever success you have, you get out of bed and earn it by your own successful behavior each and every morning. But you can't let prudent paranoia grow to govern. Fortune favors the bold. Bold with reason, but bold. Jason Marrs and I have built this book to embolden. To give you good reason to be bolder—and more creative and inventive and effective—in using price to your extreme advantage, to be as profitable as it is possible to be.

Price, Profit, Power, and Prosperity = Choice

Your prosperity begins with your price strategy.

Decisions about and presentation of price affect a great many things in a business, as you'll discover in this book. These include positioning, the kind of customers you attract, the kind of staff you attract and their attitudes, your own pride, but most importantly, profit. Profit, in turn, absolutely determines the strength or weakness, power or vulnerability your business possesses. Profit regulates power as a thermostat adjusted up or down regulates room temperature. Profit determines how bold and aggressive or timid and constrained you are in reaching out to acquire new customers or creating brand identity and awareness;

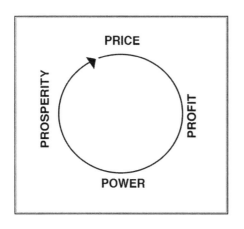

how well you can serve and satisfy customers—which affects retention, repeat business frequency, and referrals; how well you can incentivize and compensate staff in order to attract and keep the best and make managerial demands. Profit also determines if your business can withstand temporary adversity, be that road torn up in front of your store for six months or a recession lasting sixty months. Profit is power, and profit is the result of price strategy. From this, prosperity or poverty, pride or disappointment, security or endless angst. Prosperity for the business owner is created by the amount of money he can take out of his business day to day without leaving it too thinly capitalized, to, in turn, meet his lifestyle needs, live free of debt, and accumulate good assets and investments, as well as the money he may take out in a lump sum and/or on-going payments via exit down the road. Profit governs this. In a closed loop, power enables profit, and it all emanates from one source and one source only: price.

You choose your prosperity by the choices you make about price.

Although I am generally regarded as a marketing strategist, I believe I have had more far-reaching impact on more entrepreneurs by influencing their price decisions than with anything else I teach, any other advice I give, any other work I do. To that end, a story: In one of my private client mastermind groups, where 20 different entrepreneurs met for two days at a time to hash out problems and opportunities in their businesses together under my leadership, two partners presented a new service they intended to add to their existing enterprise. It could be delivered only several times a year, with a maximum of fifty customers accommodated each time, to be drawn from their thousands of existing customers now buying lesser-priced products and services. They had done some loosey-goosey research via surveys, focus groups, and analysis of similar or competitive business and determined they could charge as much as $2,000.00 per person. Most of the others in my group attacked these fellows instantly, in near unanimous and rather fervent agreement that their proposed price was way, way too low for the value of the service to the right customer (an important point) and the supply-demand ratio likely to exist given the pool of thousands to draw from. But these guys were convinced that $2,000.00 was as far as this price could possibly be stretched. The meeting ended in discord, despite my siding with the group against the partners' price belief, and making my best, reasoned argument.

Three months later, at the next meeting, these two partners presented a more fleshed out, ready to advertise version of their proposed service, and stated their firm intent to price at $2,000.00.

After another round of heated debate, I left my place at the head of conference table, went into my office with my checkbook, returned, wrote out a check to the guys for $100,000.00 ($2,000.00 x 50), slid it across the table, and said, "Enough debate. If you're locked in and happy with your $2,000.00 price, I'll buy all 50 customer positions. You deliver the service as you planned. You let me market as I please to your current customer list, I'm going to sell this at $10,000.00, and make a very nice $400,000.00 spread. Three times a year. $1.2 million. Take my check and let's shake hands on this." They refused. They went home and rather shakily rolled out their service with a daring, to them, price of $4,500.00, a 225% higher price than they'd proposed—and sold out the 50 spots quickly and easily. Today, a few years later, they sell this for $6,500.00, with an $8,500.00 deluxe option, and, at my urging, also figured out how to accommodate 100 rather than 50, and do it three times a year. Over five years, the price strategy pushed on them is worth more than $7 million above what they were committed to settling for. Truly an example of my friend Foster Hibbard's maxim: *Go to the ocean with teaspoon or bucket; the ocean doesn't care.*

This **is the power of price**. Throughout this book, you will come to understand why such a huge spread existed between what these savvy, successful entrepreneurs believed the maximum possible selling price was, and what it really was, and how to identify similarly inaccurate beliefs in your mind and uncover amazing opportunities for explosive profit improvement in your business. In this way, **this book can have million dollar or multi-million dollar importance to you, beginning immediately, with collection occurring over the next few years**. That is not empty hype. It is fact, established by the story I just told you being repeated in hundreds of different businesses, industries, and professions hundreds of times as a result of my guidance and, at times, insistence.

One such demonstration belongs to my co-author, Jason Marrs, who has a personal price strategy story that is, in many respects, much more remarkable than the one I just shared. Jason, as marketing director for his wife's large, thriving, multi-therapist professional practice in the field of education and therapy for children, competes with free services very aggressively promoted by government agencies and in partnership with the public school system, teachers, and counselors, as well as with solo-therapist private practices charging fees a fraction of his wife's. Jason has built an extraordinary, enviable, profitable business with price strategy boldly defiant of a plethora of government-imposed obstacles and cheaper and cheapest price competition. His success in this difficult environment has not gone unnoticed. Others in his field and many others outside the medical profession began asking him for his "secrets," knocking on his door for consulting, and, today, Jason is one of the foremost advisors and coaches to small business, medium-sized companies, entrepreneurs, and professionals on price strategy. After all, if you want certain survival on a camping trip, who better to recruit as your guide than a battle-scarred but successful survivor of journeys through the most dangerous jungles on earth?—in this case, the land of "free."

Together, Jason and I have a mission of liberating you from all fear or timidity toward price, and of empowering you with both courage and price-strategy competence and creativity so that you can substantially improve your business' profitability and sustainability. To this, you need to bring as open a mind as you possibly can. An intellectual willingness to re-examine your every belief about price in your business, and to adapt rather than resist proven profit strategy drawn from outside the narrow confines of your particular industry and your experience in it thus far. Today must be a new day, not a stubborn re-living of the ones before.

Notes

1. Each chapter is identified as written by Jason or me.

2. An offer of additional resources from Jason appears on page 233, one from me on page 234. You need not wait until you complete the book to take advantage of these opportunities!

3. *The opinions expressed in this book are those of the authors, not necessarily those of the publisher.* Some of these opinions are exaggerated in order to make a point, be provocative, or be humorous. The book is intended for people with a sense of humor. One of the authors' beliefs is if you don't offend somebody by noon each day, you aren't saying or doing much. We have made sure to exceed quota here. If you are easily offended and do not have a sense of humor, you probably should NOT read this book.

4. *For anyone who is gender or political-correctness sensitive, to head off letters.* The authors have predominantly used he, him, etc. throughout the book with only occasional exception, rather than awkwardly saying he or she, him or her. They do not mean this as a slight to women, only as a convenience. They are not getting paid by the word.

5. *This publication is designed to provide accurate and authoritative information in regard to the subject matter covered.* While every effort has been made to ensure factual accuracy, no warranties concerning such acts are made. This book is published for general information and entertainment purposes only. It is sold with the understanding that the publisher is not engaged in rendering legal, accounting, or other professional services. If legal advice or other expert assistance is required, the services of a competent professional person should be sought.

6. *Price laws and regulations are complex and tricky, and meddlers in your price strategy include the Federal Trade Commission,*

your state and even local government, and possibly federal or state regulatory agencies specific to your industry or profession. The authors are not lawyers (thankfully) or experts in legal matters, nor is this book intended as a substitute for legal advice of any kind. We accept no responsibility or liability of any kind—nor does the publisher or any source cited in the book—for whatever decisions you purportedly make as a result of something you read here. You can secure some price law information at www.FTC.gov, but again, other regulatory bodies may have something to say about price strategy in your field.

7. *Throughout the book you will encounter references to Glazer-Kennedy Insider's Circle™,* an international membership organization comprised of entrepreneurs, business owners, sales professionals, and self-employed professionals with a strong common interest in marketing and business development with an emphasis on maximum profit. Members have access to several different monthly newsletters, teleseminars, Q&A teleconferences with me and other experts, online courses, two conventions/conferences each year, and the kind of mastermind groups mentioned in this introduction at a national level in the United States as well as at the local level, in over 100 cities, where there are Glazer-Kennedy Insider's Circle™ local Chapters. Refer to page 234 for more information.

About the Authors

JASON MARRS is an intense innovator and pricing/marketing strategist coaching entrepreneurs and professionals to overcome price reluctance and resistance, to stop leaving untold sums of money on the table, and to finally get paid all they are worth—so they can have the freedom and security to enjoy the important things in life. He is also an in-the-trenches entrepreneur with successful business interests in healthcare, education, publishing, and consulting. Learning from champions of business' real purpose, he is unapologetic about putting his wife and two young children before all else, and living proof that business success and a happy home life can coexist.

Jason rarely takes on new private clients but does occasionally accept those he finds interesting. Inquiries should include information about industry or profession, issues, interests, and a compelling message and e-mailed to Jason's attention at: Jason@ StrategicPricingCenter.com. More information can be obtained at **www.SimplePricingSystem.com**

DAN S. KENNEDY is a multi-millionaire serial entrepreneur with past and present interests in diverse businesses; a strategic advisor, marketing consultant, and coach with a cadre of private clients ranging from exceptionally ambitious entrepreneurs to the CEO's of companies as large as $1.5 billion; one of the highest paid direct-response copywriters in the world; a popular professional speaker and seminar leader; and a prolific author. He is provocative, irreverent, and sarcastic—but most importantly, he's effective. He and his network of consultants directly influence over 1 million small business owners annually, who have kept coming back for more for 30 years. His office is in Arizona, his homes in Ohio and Virginia, he races harness horses professionally and drives in about 200 races annually, his current, third wife is also his second wife, and they share parenting of The Million Dollar Dog. As a speaker Dan has appeared repeatedly with countless celebrity-entrepreneurs like Gene Simmons (KISS), Joan Rivers, Donald Trump, Debbi Fields (Mrs. Fields Cookies), and Jim McCann (1-800-Flowers), broadcasters Larry King and the late Paul Harvey, and America's leading success and sales speakers including Zig Ziglar, Brian Tracy, and Tom Hopkins. With Zig, Dan appeared at more than 200 events, with audiences from 10,000 to 25,000 strong.

You can find information about his books at **www. NoBSBooks.com**, about Membership in Glazer-Kennedy Insider's Circle™ to which he contributes content at **www. DanKennedy.com/PriceBook**, and read his weekly political columns at **www. BusinessAndMedia.org**

Dan is available for a limited number of speaking engagements each year, as well as single and multi-day private consulting engagements, and occasionally accepts a new consulting/copywriting client in whose business he detects enormous unexploited opportunity. Direct communication with Dan can be accomplished by fax: (602) 269-3113.

About the Guest Contributors

DARIN SPINDLER is a marketing consultant and specialist in lead generation and online marketing for independent and franchised brick-and-mortar local businesses. His systems have created well over 5 million new customers for local business owners coast to coast. Types of businesses now participating in Darin's nationwide new customer development programs go far beyond the original bowling centers to include restaurants and taverns, movie theaters, golf courses, learning centers, hair salons, tanning salons, health clubs, fitness centers, health care practices, home remodeling contractors, dry cleaners, and over 50 other categories. He works closely with Dan Kennedy in development and operation of "done-for-them" lead generation marketing systems for these businesses. Complete information and, of course, a compelling Free can be found at: www. NewLocalCustomersNow.com/Kennedy

DR. BARRY A.S. LYCKA, M.D., FRCPC, is a prominent physician, lecturer, business consultant, and mentor to other physicians worldwide, including those participating in his private coaching/ mastermind groups. Information for doctors and other business owners is available at www.aestheticprofits.com/mastermind; for everyone at www.WellAndWiseOnline.com. Dr. Lycka can be reached at www.BarryLyckaMD.com. He is also a contributor to several other Dan Kennedy books, including *Uncensored Sales Strategies* by Sydney Biddle Barrows and Dan Kennedy; *No B.S. Marketing to the Affluent*; and *The Ultimate Marketing Plan*.

DEAN KILLINGBECK is a popular speaker, available to talk to groups of business owners about smarter, more sophisticated marketing. He is the owner of New Customers Now!, located in Howell, Michigan, providing turnkey direct-mail campaigns for many different kinds of businesses. He is also a specialist in birthday-offers and birthday-card mailings, to existing customers and as outreach to new customers. For a copy of his free report, "How To Get Good New Customers, Even In Tough Times, When Competitors Can't," visit www.NewCustomersNowMarketing.com.

SECTION I

CHAPTER 1

Price and Fee
Failures

Dan Kennedy

There are many ways to fail at price strategy. Here is a short list:

1. Pricing by textbook formulas, industry norms, or other "standard" means
2. Excess concern about competitors' lower prices
3. Attracting customers who buy by price
4. Pre-determined belief system about "what they'll pay"
5. Permitting apples-to-apples comparisons
6. Insufficient differentiation
7. Not offering premium price options
8. Ignorance or stupidity about "business math"
9. Poor self-esteem/business-esteem; feelings of not deserving more

These and others are explored throughout the book.

One of the most unpleasant discoveries to be made here has to do with your own thinking, rather than with specific price strategy. After all, what war strategy could be useful to a true conscientious objector, opposed to killing for any reason, under any circumstances? That's a guy you do not want in your foxhole, watching your back! You don't want a conscientious objector to highest-price-and-profits-possible running a business for you either. Hopefully, that's not you!

If you came to these pages hoping for little tricks, like whether to say 50% off, half off, or 2 for 1, you're in for disappointment, or hopefully, a change of heart. [That sort of thing is tactics, not strategy.] We are about something much bigger than that. This book is, first and foremost, about challenging all your pre-conceived, present ideas about price—most importantly, about the limits of the prices you can successfully command. Second, based on the first, our objective is to have you alter your strategic approach to price, and view it within the context of marketing, not as a separate task tied to price-book and calculator.

Most business owners are failures at price strategy, to an extent they are unaware of. That ignorance might be bliss, but it's very costly and hazardous to one's wealth.

When I say they fail at price strategy, I mean that they fail to use price as a positive marketing tool and path to advantage. I also mean that they fail to create the greatest possible profit in their business. The reasons for these failures group into attitudinal and practical; into fear-based ideas and self-imposed limitations; and into marketing and selling mistakes. The most important thing to know going in is that your prices are your choice and your responsibility. Even in situations where most would believe price was imposed—like Jason's business, where he and his wife compete as a premium-priced, private provider against free services funded for consumers by the government—there is always opportunity for liberation and control, by acceptance of responsibility.

There's an old, not very funny joke about two construction workers perched side by side on a girder, at lunch break. One opens his lunchbox and cries out in frustration and rage, spews curses, and says "Damn, damn, damn, I can't stand this—cheese sandwiches again. All I ever get are cheese sandwiches!" The other guy says: "Why don't you ask your wife to make you something different?" Sadly, the first fellow mumbles "I pack my own lunch."

If you are self-employed, a business owner, in professional practice, or a sales professional, you write your own paycheck. If you're not satisfied with it, you know who to complain to. But the amount on the paycheck is pre-ordained long before it is actually inked. It begins with your price strategy. And that is preceded by your belief system about price. That likely affected by your belief system about money and wealth and success.

I hope you've arrived here with an open mind, a creative spirit, and a sincere determination to write yourself out much, much bigger paychecks.

Be careful of argument with or hasty rejection of anything you read here that is in conflict with your existent beliefs, but is about pursuit of bigger paychecks. You can't expect to stay married to the exact same thinking and beliefs about price, and to the same strategy about price, but somehow magically see larger dollar amounts on your paychecks. You will be tempted to argue and quickly reject what is presented here. The temptation is perfectly understandable, yet you must be alert for it and then fight it with all your will. Force your mind to be open. Nothing less will do!

The Ultimate Failure

Other than going out of business entirely and slinking off into the sunset, tail beneath your legs, in search of a hiding place—such as an ordinary j-o-b—the next worst failure is staying in business but still slinking about with tail beneath your legs, settling for table scraps-level income when a king's feast-type income was within reach.

To be fair about this, there are a lot of people who own businesses who are there because of non-financial motivations, typically an interest in the work in the business and a distaste for having a boss. To these folks, adequate income is perfectly satisfactory, maximum income of no interest. They can hoist the banner of "Mission Accomplished" and declare themselves successful as long as the bills are paid at the shop and at home. But a great many more settle for only adequate rather than exceptional income, and just making a living rather than developing wealth because they believe it's all they can reasonably expect their business to provide, and in doing so, they sell it and themselves very short—and, whether they have clarity about it or not, they are failures. I know that is harsh. But if you have scaled back, down-sized, and surrendered your original and early ambitions to a lesser level of achievement, you live in failure. If you leave profit and other opportunity capable of fulfilling the original ambition lying right on the table in front of you thanks to poor, uncorrected vision, or fear and timidity, or just about any other untreated but treatable handicap, sorry, but you live in failure.

I am a devoted, dedicated, passionate champion of the independent business owner and entrepreneur, and of the sales warriors. Without us, it's all over. Almost any other occupational groups could take a few months off and the nation might survive. If we all slept for a week, collapse would be complete. Because we risk while others trade all for seeming safety; because we invest while others squander; because we innovate while others are complacent; because we work twice the hours and with ten times the intensity than the overwhelming majority who prefer 9-to-5; because we take on infinitely more responsibility; because we get bruised and bloodied and knocked down and get back in the game while others sit in the bleachers; because we pay a grossly disproportionate share of all taxes and act as Atlas carrying the rest of the population on our shoulders; and because we create and organize and deliver goods, services, experiences, and value while others consume, we deserve ultimate prosperity, which requires making our businesses and business activities as profitable as they can possibly be, letting not even a cent that might have been in our coffers somehow escape. You have both right and responsibility to get all the profit-produced prosperity you can squeeze from your business. Not a drop less.

This is _not_ greed. Greed is defined in the dictionary as *selfish* desire. There is profound difference between self-interest and selfishness. If you are unfamiliar with the distinction or, worse, inhibited by that misunderstanding, I urge you to read three books as quickly as you can: the novel *Atlas Shrugged* by Ayn Rand, the book *Thou Shall Prosper* by Rabbi Daniel Lapine, and my own *No B.S. Wealth Attraction in The New Economy*. I am advocating to you the proper, appropriate, deserved obtainment of all that is for you, to be derived by fair exchange of value—recognizing the admittedly uncommon but demonstrable (and demonstrated in this book) fact that there can be value to the consumer in a merchant's premium, above-par prices. If you live the ultimate failure of deriving less profit than possible from your providing goods and/or services of value, you do not win a merit badge for reduction of greed by self-imposed restraint. There is no such merit badge, as the act is without merit.

I lack the space and time here to even try to convince you of this liberating, empowering philosophy—this is a book of mechanical, not philosophical instruction. That's what you bought and that is what you are going to get. But the tools in this toolbox will be of greatly diminished value to you without the wholehearted embrace of a capitalistic, self-interest-based, guilt-free philosophy about prosperity. So, again, I urge reading the above-mentioned books in tandem with this one.

The opposite of the ultimate failure is the ultimate success of living your life exactly and entirely as you choose, facilitated by your business working for you (not you for it) as needed, and as part of that, manufacturing every possible profit.

CHAPTER 2

Discounting
Without Damage

Jason Marrs

I wasn't raised like most kids. Even from kids who grew up in business like I did, my family had a different way of doing things. It is not surprising though. My mother was not very far removed from tremendous wealth. To put it into perspective, my grandmother went to college in California during the Great Depression. Considering that was a time before college was popular, that she was female, and that she came from rural New Mexico says a lot about the family's financial resources.

Our family was not highly motivated by the advertising of a SALE! A lesson that I was always taught was not to get overly excited about sale prices because nine times out of ten, you can always buy the item for that price. That has been a good lesson for me. I have found it to be the case. Sale prices are often nothing more that statements of what you should really be paying for something. And that is the downside to discounts. They can destroy price integrity with blinding speed. On the other hand they can bring a stampede of buyers through the door faster than just about anything else.

It is no wonder discounts and I have such an uneasy relationship. On one hand I hate them because they can be such a destructive force. On the other hand I love them because they are such an effective way to drive sales. I think you should share my uneasy relationship with discounts, even if you don't share my childhood-ingrained skepticism of them as a consumer. Most business owners use discounts too casually and thoughtlessly, and too often, because they like the positive effects and do not fully understand the negative effects.

The thing to keep in mind is that offering discounts is a form of selling on price. When you offer a discount you are taking the focus from the value you provide and placing it squarely on your price. There is no way to escape that. To maintain higher prices you have to be adept at selling value. Discounts erode your ability to do that. Any reduction in prices can damage your price integrity. Later, getting the same customer to stop thinking about price and re-focus on value can prove difficult.

Not only that, studies show that discounts actually reduce the effectiveness of whatever is being discounted. By that I mean that the discounted offering literally does not perform as well as it did at full price. That sounds impossible, but double blind studies using prescription drugs and OTC health products, cosmetics, and other products have shown this to be true. A study conducted by a group of resort properties matched their most glowing comment cards to the guests paying full price or nearly full price, the most critical comment cards to guests who had bought at deeply discounted rates and knew it. Part of the

Price Orgasms

The folks at the California Institute of Technology hooked 20 people up to MRI-type brain scans while having them taste wine. They told them that they were tasting five different Cabernet Sauvignons, each priced differently. In truth, they were given two twice, one once. A $90.00 wine was served marked once with its real price but once as a $10.00 wine, while another served twice was marked once as a cheap $5.00 wine, and again marked as a $45.00 wine. The test subjects' scanned brains unanimously displayed more pleasure when tasting the wines they believed to be higher priced than when tasting the wines believed to be lowest in price. Their expectations based on stated price—and belief in the truthfulness of the prices—influenced, even controlled the relative pleasure experienced. (And later, when given the same wines with no price markings just to sample and choose, they all rated the $5.00 wine as better than the others!) Your tax dollars at work—funding from the National Science Foundation. I have always thought the ride of a Mercedes terribly hard and uncomfortable and figured people believe it's better than it is because it has to be, since it's a Mercedes, but I'll bet if you blindfolded 'em and drove them around in a Mercedes and told them that it was a Ford, and in a Ford and told them that it was a Mercedes, you'd get a different reaction. *(Dan Kennedy. Source: Yahoo News 1-14-08)*

explanation for that may be that the discounted rates drew a poorer quality customer. That would not surprise me—in my health care business, I deliberately try to repel clients concerned with price and discounts. But it also suggests that in the same way that people told they were taking a more expensive drug expected and got better outcomes, the guests paying substantially higher rates expected a better experience and molded their assessment to their expectation.

Ironically, discounts can also lead to dissatisfaction in your clientele. Discounts can lead your clients to ask themselves why your price can be discounted. They look at the price they have been paying, and then they look at the discount and smell a rat. They wonder why they can't get that price some other time. If they recently paid full price for a product now put on sale, they feel cheated. This is why it is so imperative that you always give a good reason for a discount and that your rules are solid. Unless you plan to compete on price continuously, then you can't have predictable sales or flexible terms. If there's a sale, it has got to be for a specific reason with specific rules.

Discounts can be a great way to modify behavior. Volume discounts are an example of this. They make sense in the buyer's mind. We are trained to expect that the more we buy the cheaper things will get. So customers are generally not skeptical or resentful if you give this type of discount. The same goes for prepay discounts and bundles. Prepay will help to keep your accounts receivable current while bundles can increase your transaction size. Businesses with seasonal slumps can disclose that as a reason for discounts at a specific time of year, with few negative ramifications. A good "reason why" can mitigate damage to overall price integrity, reputation, and relationship with regular customers, and can create the kind of behavior you want from the customer—such as buying now, not later; during off-season; bigger quantities.

As for using discounts to bring new customers through the door, my suggestion is to have something that is designed to be *the* thing that you use to drive traffic. By doing that, you can isolate the damage discounting will do to your price integrity. You can, if you wish, preserve full, fixed pricing for all products and services other than that one thing you periodically discount during new customer promotional campaigns, or perpetually discount for that purpose if you must.

Free as The Enemy?

Dan calls FREE the most powerful word in the English language. He's right. But I'd like to add that FREE is also the most hypocritical word in the English language. Nothing is free. Everything must be paid for by someone, somehow. If nothing else there is always a cost of time, intelligence, privacy, or quality. Admittedly the digital world has blurred that line. However, it has not erased it. There is no doubt that FREE is a powerful word. The word FREE can generate a lot of traffic. The word FREE can get buyers off of the fence. The word FREE can even get people to take action purely to get something free that they have absolutely no interest in.

Like all powerful things, FREE has a dark side. The word FREE has destructive force, because it can create expectation of more free and more free after that, literally downgrading buyers to mooches, and creating barriers to you ever (or ever again) selling value and being properly paid for it.

You hear the cries, "we won't pay for it," "we'll get it someplace else for free." The news media is currently being browbeaten with that mantra while Rupert Murdoch and some other newspaper owners try desperately to charge for what they have been giving away. The irony of the news media is that many once charged for their online content, but then removed the price in favor of giving it away for free since there was no extra cost for posting it to their websites. Oops. It's hard to walk that one back. The news media is a cautionary tale of which every business should take note. They confused the costs of their print editions with the value that they provided. They lost sight of the fact that their value should be based on the information they provide regardless of the medium used to distribute it. Predictably, this mistake has destroyed the value of the information they provide. It has also reinvigorated the entitlement junkies' demands for free.

Of course this is not a new phenomenon. Back in the '70s people actually rioted over having to pay for concerts. They demanded that the music be free. They had no concern for the time and energy the musicians put into creating the music. They put no thought into the cost of the venue, the electricity, the development of the music, or the countless other expenses required to put on a show.

Now we find ourselves moving into a new era of problems with FREE permeating our society. In Queens, New York, a group of kids repeatedly stabbed a bus driver because they wanted a free ride. In Florida, a cop was fired because he repeatedly demanded free coffee from Starbucks; store employees finally complained that he came in several times a night cutting the line and demanding coffee for free. President Obama got himself elected by promising to give a lot of things away for free. This is a widespread and growing problem. In Greece, Spain, even in Puerto Rico, rioters fill the streets protesting small cuts in the benefits government workers and retirees have been receiving for free. In a Midwest city last year, a pizza chain ran an outright free pizza promotion and had thousands—on a work day—lined up in cars, requiring four- and five-hour waits. When the stores ran out of pizza, fights broke out, several cars were lit on fire, and people were hurt and taken to hospitals. When Oprah gave away free cars to her audience, they were vocally unhappy and several threatened lawsuits upon discovery they owed taxes on the gifts.

We marketers feed this by offering more and more things for free. That's why you need to be extremely careful how you use the word free. Using FREE is a dangerous and slippery slope and you need to recognize that. FREE trains buyers to not only expect things to be free, but to demand it. To make matters worse, as the news media has learned, people do not value free. You have got to be very, very careful when using free.

It seems like everywhere I look FREE is being used without regard to consequences. In fact, I'd like to take this space to make a bold prediction. I predict a day of reckoning is coming to some very well known internet marketers if they don't change their ways. If you have paid any attention to internet marketing you undoubtedly know what I am talking about. It seems like every week there is someone giving away what they once charged three thousand dollars for. You have to have seen the pitches: "When this was released six months ago, it sold for $2,997.00 and 50,000 copies of this sold out in 3 minutes, but you can get it for free by entering your name and e-mail in the form below right now." If they did sell 50,000 at $2,997.00, will those buyers ever trust them again after seeing it given away for free? This is a strategy called Skimming (see Chapter 17), but carried to extraordinary extreme. If they did not actually sell it at the price they claim, they are lying, and liars are always eventually exposed. They would also be running afoul of the law.

Giving away something that was once priced at a premium will devalue it and all your other offers. It will erode trust. It will train buyers to expect that which is $2,997.00 today will be free tomorrow. I have taken several up on their free offers. They would be much better off giving away highlights of the original program as opposed to the whole thing. A highlights program would still have caché but it would not degrade price integrity since it never had a price. Done right it could even lead to more sales of the original product. Giving away a premium offering for free degrades its perceived value. To make matters worse, the more recently it had a premium price, the more likely giving it away for free will compromise the price integrity of the other offerings by the same business. I'm sure the guys who are doing this have convinced themselves otherwise, but they are wrong. I don't care how fast this grows your list, I don't care if you think you are triggering reciprocity, you are degrading the quality and viability of your buyers by giving away a premium offering for free. You are not, I repeat not, building trust or loyalty. You are building discontent and sowing the seeds of hatred. Watch the long-term behavior; it will deteriorate just as it has for the news media. As the old saying goes, why buy the cow if you can get the milk for free?

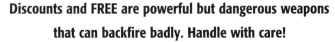

NO B.S. Price Strategy Warning #1

Discounts and FREE are powerful but dangerous weapons that can backfire badly. Handle with care!
There are ways to use them profitably, and times and places where you must use them, but thoughtful concern for the consequences is always required.

With all that said, FREE used thoughtfully, carefully, and sparingly, or with a standard new customer offer, or in ways that do not degrade product previously sold at full price without a very good reason palatable to all, can be a powerful business-builder. (You will find mine in an offer to you on page 233 and Dan's on page 234.)

I do not believe you can simply swear off free—or discounts, for that matter. Despite personal biases, I strive to adapt to the evolving culture of free in ways that help rather than harm my businesses and my clients' businesses, and you should too. Darwin taught us that the survivors were not necessarily the strongest, but those most able to adapt to current conditions. Having enormous market share and deep pockets does not exempt you from extinction.

The music industry is learning this the hard way. They have long viewed MP3s, file sharing, and piracy as threats despite the fact that these threats were expanding the overall market. So instead of figuring out how to capitalize on the revolution that is happening they have been wasting critical resources on a war they can't win. The sacred cow of the traditional record label will be slaughtered. They need to evolve. We all do. Again, this is why it is so important to challenge how you see things. Free is no different. You have to constantly ask yourself if you should fight the battle, join in the use of FREE, or leave altogether. You have to contemplate if you should entrench and try to protect your cash cow, or sacrifice it. If you should sacrifice it, what are the new opportunities? We don't get the answers to those questions without challenging our beliefs.

I had to challenge my belief about participating with free. As much as I hate it, I had to come to terms with the fact that I can use it. Most of us do. We give certain things away while charging for others. Maybe it's a bonus, maybe it is a sample, maybe it is free information such as a blog post or an e-zine, but free is there and being used. Free is not going away anytime soon. It and the expectation of it is expanding. If you ignore it or deny the threat it poses to your current business model, you do so at your own peril. If you ignore it or deny the opportunities it offers, you operate under a handicap.

"Never discount. Never free." is impossibly stubborn, but for very, very, very few providers of elite professional services to very small numbers of elite clients. "Always/often discount. A lot for free, all the time" is a high-risk game, too high-risk for my taste, and historically, consistently, a path to a cliff's edge from which there's no retreat.

Can Free Be Your Ally?

It is easy to feel dismayed or even helpless when thinking about free. It is hard to imagine competing with it let alone providing it but still profiting.

Using free can be tricky. If you start off free and then try to move to paid, at worst you will have an angry list that revolts; at best you will have poor results. If you have a premium offering then you give it away, you will devalue it and everything else you offer. Free is a fickle mistress. It seems there is nothing you can do to please her. Such is the nature of powerful things. Free is a force to be reckoned with. It is pervasive and evolving. It's like using dynamite. It has a purpose. There is a time and place for using it. You just have to be very careful with it.

That poses the question, how do you use free without destroying your business? The answer to that question tends to be unique to each type of business. If you have something addictive or habit forming you could give away samples. Drug dealers have long used this tactic. So have vendors on the food court at the mall. The main reason they hand you teriyaki chicken on a toothpick is because they hope you'll love the taste so much you'll buy it. There's also a reciprocity component. Unfortunately, that strategy won't work for everyone. While the local sandwich shop can give away free samples of food without any risk of damaging their price integrity, a high-end restaurant such as Morton's would not be able to get away with it so easily. And when it comes to someone such as Dan or me, we can't give away samples of our consulting without damaging our ability to command premium fees. We can *demonstrate* our wizardry, though, in seminar environments where everyone has paid to be there, and we can carefully give away some information in media, free or deeply discounted as with this book.

This is something every business can do, as demonstration of expertise or value, at deep discount or for free, that does little damage. For almost every business, I've become a fan of giving away information since it can be created once and given to a lot of people over and over again. I like free newsletters, information packages, booklets, and even websites. I'm not talking about information that negates your customer's need to use you. I'm talking about information that helps educate the customer. Information that helps the customer understand key issues and identify if they belong in your camp or someplace else. I call this *edu-marketing*.

I say that like it is a new thing, but it's not. Companies have been using educational campaigns to gently woo customers since the dawn of commerce. However, it is growing more advanced now. Educating your buyers helps to cut through the traditional advertising clutter. It builds trust. It allows you to get your point across and create more informed buyers. Every business has things that are important for the buyer to know. Give these things away. Use them to improve the market. I prefer an educated buyer. When you have an educated buyer they "get it," They understand what they are supposed to do. They are far more apt to help you maximize your ability to help them.

On the other hand, an uninformed buyer will be much more prone to sabotage your efforts due to their lack of understanding. That is the natural response to not knowing what you are doing. This happens because when we don't know what we are doing we operate with something called the Executive Mind. The Executive Mind is our conscious thinking brain. It is only able to process and handle a limited amount of information because it is trying to create a map for the Habitual Mind to follow in the future. The Habitual Mind is the mind we use when we're "in the zone." It is the mind we want our customers using when they come to us. We want them to know what they want and have an idea of what it takes to get there. We want them to understand and not be confused.

Again, I'm not talking about giving away the farm. I am talking about giving away the basic foundational information and ideas that buyers need to make informed decisions. Every business has this information. Every business should be using this to their advantage.

Tell me, what do I need to know to do business with you? What do I need to know to feel confident about deciding to place my trust in you? How will I know I'm right for you and you are right for me? Once you answer those questions, you can advertise that information to people who will take you up on it. It will build your credibility and will give you the opportunity to convert them to buyers. This is something any business can and should do.

Two Things You Should NEVER Do

"Never" is a very strong word. It's rarely advisable to use it. But in these two instances, I feel so strongly about the advice I'll risk the permanent, no exceptions ban.

1. **If you have a prestige offering, do not give it away for free**. There is nothing prestigious about free. There is no faster way to dilute your ability to charge a high price than by giving it away. **Also be careful about offering it at discounts**. Even that can destroy its price integrity. Protect prestige. If you find you need extra "juice" to sell that product, add value to it with stronger or more dramatic warranties, bonuses, and premiums, a special event for all who buy it during the promotional period, financing. But don't sacrifice its price outright.

2. **If you must discount, must put items on sale or must promote free offers, don't be predictable**. This is the only way to negate training people to expect something. If you do the same thing at the same time, every time, you train them. Once you train them to expect something you have to deliver it or you sow the seeds of discontent. If they come to realize you advertise at full price for three weeks, then discount the fourth, they'll wait; if you stop the discounting, they won't buy at all. If you run a Half-Price Sale every July, customers will sit on their hands in May and June. If you frequently discount, they'll lose all faith in real prices and buy only when you run sales, then build up immunity to that, forcing you to conceive bigger sales with bigger discounts and more free gifts.

CHAPTER 3

If and When You Discount, Get Quid Pro Quo

Dan Kennedy

I am in general agreement with Jason about all the evils of discounting. This does not necessarily preclude my use of discounting, for my own businesses or for clients, but it makes me wary and reluctant, and motivates me to try and get something in exchange.

A simple exchange of value might be immediate response. In marketing seminars, for example, there is often an early registration discount tied to a set deadline. I will come right out and say: "If we have to keep chasing you and sending you mailing after mailing after mailing, we'll eventually get you (you know you want and need to come), but we will have spent a lot of time and money. Better to give that to you as savings in exchange for your earliest registration." This has two virtues.

One, it provides a reason for the offered discount, which is some buffer against cheapening of the product or the thought that the retail price is simple fiction. Two, it has a ring of truth, because, in this case, there *is* real truth in the justification of the discount.

Years ago, when I was engaged in person-to-person, face-to-face selling of a particular product, I found myself running up against last minute price resistance. I succeeded with the strategy of "pulling the discount rabbit out of my hat"—conditional on the buyer assisting me with referrals to secure appointments with at least two friends, neighbors, or colleagues. That dates back to the 1970s, and I first learned it from Howard Bonnell, then a sales management executive with the World Book Encyclopedia Company, and from Paul J. Meyer, the founder of Success Motivation Institute, who gave a talk about perpetuating an "endless chain of referrals." Very recently, I spotted an item in *Entrepreneur* magazine about a similar strategy, referring to an electrical contractor who, after closing the sale reveals a lower available price, if the customer will fill out referral postcards to be sent to the neighbors, right then and there.

In my consulting/copywriting practice, as of this writing, my base daily fee is $18,800.00, and copywriting project fees are calculated by multiplying that times the number of days I estimate will be required. Ten days = a fee of $188,000.00. I sometimes discount the daily consulting fee for a client booking consecutive days back to back or pre-booking multiple days spaced through the same calendar year, with reason given that I am getting value from that client in exchange for the discount; either time efficiency or the convenience of filling the calendar and not needing to worry about getting more clients. I sometimes discount the copywriting fee if I am getting several projects all related to the same product to do at the same time, with reason given: time efficiency—the same research supports all the projects, some of the copy written for one migrates to three.

These are, in essence, quantity discounts, but with more elegant reason given. The one thing I never, never, never do is discount fees purely because of the client's desire to negotiate or some competitive pressure. Never, without good reason featuring some quid pro quo.

Money at a Discount

In the above example, the idea of a $188,000.00 fee for copywriting work might shock you. And if it were being paid by the client simply for a few days of copywriting work, i.e., for the time or the labor, it would be outrageous. He could hire his own copywriter as a full-time employee to be underfoot forty hours a week every week for a year for that sum. But for me, it's relatively routine because I'm not charging for time or labor; I'm charging to develop an asset the client will own, that will yield dividends over time far beyond the initial investment. For example, if, for that fee, he obtained an ad campaign driving prospects to a website where they read a sales letter and bought his products that he used for the next five years, that amortizes the fee to $37,600.00 a year. And if it sells $500,000.00 of goods each year, that's $2.5-million across its five-year life, a return on investment of almost 1,400%. Or: a discount of $2.3 million; the buying of money at a huge discount. This is what intelligent businesspeople try to accomplish anytime they pay for expertise; buy money at a good discount. And, just how many times would *you* like to buy something for $188,000.00 that will yield $2.5-million over five years?

There are actually two price strategies in play in the above paragraph's explanation of my fees: first, apples to oranges comparison (see the end of Chapter 13); second, selling money at a discount. The second can even lend itself to visual demonstration. For a speaker selling a moneymaking program to seminar audiences, I fashioned the exercise by calling for volunteers, picking three, bringing them up on stage, and having them bid to buy $100.00 bills—high bidder getting the $100.00 bill. Usually, some goof bid a dollar, another twenty dollars or so, some wiz bid ninety-nine dollars. He would give the high bidder the $100.00 bill, then pull out a giant roll of hundreds, say he would average the bids to, say fifty, and invite all who wanted in on the deal to "come on down"!—then quickly stop the madness, get everybody back in their seats, and explain that his proposition to own his system was even better, because they'd be turning a few hundred dollars into hundreds of thousands of dollars in just the next twelve months. Show of hands, how many would bid at least $1,000.00 on a briefcase containing one thousand of the $100-bills (photo shown on screen) , thus paying only one dollar for each $100? **This took all the focus of the audience off his price and fixated it on the large gain to be had. The price was now** *felt* **as a huge discount rather than as a stiff price for the product,** which consisted of some audio CDs, manuals, and an online coaching program; the whole thing fit into a single three-ring notebook.

Back to the quid pro quo: to let somebody have a product like this, purported to be worth $100,000.00 this year and again next year and the year after that for the small price of just $1,000.00 makes no sense. Franchises sell for 50 times that much and then require even more investment, risk, and working 60 hours a week. This discount must be made rational. In this case, several reasons were given, the specifics of which are not important here, but the fact that they were given, vital.

The Something-In-Exchange Split-Test

In direct marketing, there is the all-important split-test, where just one variable is tested, "A" against "B." That might be price

---

or the ad's headline or two different photos or any other element. Some years back, I had a regional chain of optical stores as a client. We ran a "Sizzling Summer Sales Event," with customers getting a pair of prescription-lens sunglasses free when purchasing a regular pair of glasses, plus a family pass to a popular area water park as a free bonus. For its time, it was an extremely generous, enticing offer. I worried it might be too good to be trusted, absent some quid pro quo. So we tested one change in the advertising in one market vs. the same advertising in the other: in one, we added the requirement that the customer bring a donation of two canned food items or at least $10.00 cash for the local food banks; in the other, no such charity connection or requirement. The results were so much better with the charitable donation requirement that no argument was possible. It mattered.

As I was writing this, a popular, national menswear chain was advertising the rather preposterous offer of "buy 1 suit, get a 2nd suit and a sports-jacket free." I bet I could improve response by making those customers bring in a used article of clothing to donate to Goodwill. Doing so would do good, too, by the way. Why not help out a charity and let it boost your sales?

CHAPTER 4

The Nasty Cancer
of FREE

Dan Kennedy

istorically, FREE has been one of the most powerful words in advertising. **It still is, but it is also become the bane of existence to many of us**, particularly those of us dealing in intellectual properties—like this book, home study courses and other education, or entertainment product like music, comedy, and movies. A destructive sense of entitlement in general, entitlement to free to be specific, and entitlement to free if cost of delivery is free—regardless of investment in creation—to be very specific is metastasizing through the consumer culture. It is most pervasive among young consumers rather than boomers or seniors. For example, a 2010 study by a major research firm (Piper Jaffray) revealed that only 40% of teens legally purchase music online, with 57% admitting they acquire pirated music from peer-to-peer networks and see nothing wrong with doing so. The percentage willing to pay up to 99-cents to download a song from a legal source dropped from 25% to 18% in just one year.

A must-read book about the culture of free, and its current and potential impact on various businesses, is appropriately titled *FREE*, by Chris Anderson. I do not agree with all the author's conclusions, but highly recommend thinking through all the questions he raises and the trends, evolving and predicted, he brings up as they may apply to or even mandate reinvention of your business.

Overall trends in American culture have affected and do affect both price and presentation of price. My grandparents lived in a pay-as-you-go culture. With very rare exception, they saved up to make major purchases and simply did without until they had accumulated enough money. Piggy banks, Mason jars, and coffee cans labeled with the purpose of their savings were common sights on kitchen counters—one for Vacation, another for Washing Machine, another for Back To School Clothes. Virtually every bank promoted Christmas Club accounts, to which deposits were made weekly all year long, for withdrawal only on the Friday immediately following Thanksgiving, the official start of the holiday shopping season. Most stores borrowed the idea with their own layaway plans, where you made weekly or monthly payments toward the purchase of a product in advance of getting it. Some smart merchants injected a little price strategy into that, by matching every dollar the customer put in with a dime, providing the plan was kept in force to completion and product ultimately purchased. The few things for which consumer credit was commonly used, notably homes and automobiles, were viewed by most as necessary evils and required 20% or higher down payments. And home buyers lived for the day of their backyard mortgage-burning party, with family and friends invited. This entire scene must seem a silly fiction to many reading this. But real people really lived this way. Honest. My very own father, after coming home from the Army, rode a little Briggs and Stratton motor scooter—not motorcycle; motor *scooter*—to and from work for over a year while he and mother saved up coins in a can for the big down-payment on a car.

In that culture, price was very real, because it was almost always paid in cash, with money saved up over time. Even Friday night out for pizza and a movie was the result of setting aside money for a couple weeks in advance. There was a reality-based mindset about money and therefore about price. That's why your grandparents can accurately recall and report the exact price they paid for many things big and small—car or gallon of gas in a given year, while today's consumer often can't tell you

A Different Time

In 1973, the year I graduated from high school, here were the prices for the following:

Average New Home	$32,500.00
Average New Car	$3,950.00
Average Rent	$175.00/month
Harvard Tuition	$3,000.00/year
Movie Ticket	$1.75
Postage Stamp	.10
Gas	.40/gallon
Coffee	$1.00/lb.

the price paid for much of anything since it happened with a thoughtless swipe of a card, or in payments for which the total price, interest included, isn't known because it's irrelevant. Even I can tell you the prices I paid for my first three cars, in 1972, 1973, and 1975, but I can no longer recall the price of the ones I bought after that. I bought the first two for cash, the third with a hefty, saved-up down-payment, a 24-month loan (the longest then possible was 36), and a co-signer. The ones after were bought much less thoughtfully or arduously, pretty much just signing my name.

My parents lived in a cultural transition from pay-as-you-go to go-now, pay-later, over time. Gradually, attitudes about credit and debt changed, and expansive use of credit not just for home and car, but furnishings, backyard pool, trips, clothes and gifts became the fast-growing normal and accepted way of life. Marketers quickly capitalized on the opportunity to shift focus from price as reasonable or fair or competitive, to monthly payments you could afford. In a relatively short period of time, we went from very little bought on credit and debt feared and loathed to much bought on credit and debt accepted with little question or angst.

My generation went all the way. We buy everything down to our morning coffee and doughnut at the 7–11 with credit and think nothing of it. We wouldn't dream of delaying a washer and dryer for three years and trekking to the laundromat while saving up money for that purchase, if we have a credit card that will take the hit. Consequently, in a great many product categories, price is not much of an issue, and sometimes not even mentioned; instead only the monthly payment matters. We are now not just a society of consumers rather than producers, but we are a debt-based society rather than an ownership-based society. Given the quick obsolescence of much of what is bought on extended payments, most people actually own next to nothing, ever, and are renting everything, although most do not think of their situation in those terms.

Along the way, a parallel cultural conversion took place. My grandparents' generation subscribed to self-reliance as secular religion. Any hand-out was shameful. They knew there was never a free lunch. As interesting side note, the earliest attempts by marketers to offer senior citizen discounts or have seniors enroll in discount plans fell flat; seniors considered it an insult to suggest they couldn't pay their way and needed a subsidy because of their age. My parents' generation gradually embraced a less rigid allegiance to "if it is to be, it is up to me" and became more accepting of, then slowly eager for government expansion and liberal philosophy. Today, the secular religion of self-reliance is as antique as pay as you go; in its place, a fast-growing, politically encouraged lust for unearned goodies, benefits, support and assistance, transfer of responsibility—to the point of entitlement.

Now, with pay-as-you-go a quaint historical footnote, go-now-and-pay-later the foundation of most consumer purchasing, the internet as a commoditizing force, and an overall cultural shift from independence to entitlement, **everything related to price is impacted, and broadly, price is under pressure.** This is more than an abstract dissertation of societal change or disintegration and political power expansion. It gets right to how Herb and Susan think about prices, payments, what they should have to pay for this or that, and what they should just be given or given access to without paying for it at all.

It's very interesting to look at media. All TV was once free. But consumers were convinced they should be willing to pay for more, more diverse, better, and "adult" TV, and cable subscriptions went from odd luxury to something most now think of as essential. Moving people from free radio to paid radio has not been nearly as successful. I say that with sorrow;

I own stock in Sirius. But even while consumers seem evermore willing to pay for TV, via cable, satellite, hulu.com TV replays, pay-per-view, they are revolting against paying for news media, particularly newspapers, prepared by real journalists with professional research; counting Tommy's blog from Mom's basement as equivalent and demanding *The New York Times* give their content free or go away altogether. Their demands—and weak-kneed publishers' acquiescence—are driving prices of books, magazines, and music into the dumpster. Even in one category like this, customers will pay for one version but insist another version should be free.

The new entitlement mentality does not stop within the borders of media and product drawn from intellectual property. A substantial percentage of people now think of health care as a right, not as products and services—so any price is viewed with hostility by many. Pensions sufficient to support oneself well throughout 30+ years of retirement, once thought of as something carrying price tags, that you bought from banks and insurance companies by saving and prudent money management, are now widely viewed as a right to which all are equally entitled regardless of what the individual has done to get educated, to advance in a career or business, to save responsibly. No less than the Ben of Ben & Jerry's Ice Cream has suggested that everybody's income be capped by law not to exceed the salary paid the President, with all the overage confiscated and re-distributed according to need, to grace all with equal amounts of these basic entitlements: food, housing, health care, retirement. Thus, entire industries and professions are threatened deeply by this attitudinal trend. All are undermined to one degree or another.

Strategically, for your business, you need to use everything provided here to its maximum advantage in your situation or a better situation you choose and craft for yourself. Very candidly, you may be in a segment of a business so threatened by these trends that you should exit and apply your talents, skills, energy, and resources elsewhere. Whatever field of enterprise you are in, seeking out buyers willing to pay for value rather than those seeking value far in excess of payment or, worse, feeling entitled to value far in excess of payment, or worst, willing to steal to avoid any payment, is critical. Being able to position yourself in a category of one for certain desirable customers, critical. Creating immunity to downward price pressure, critical.

Immune systems are always multi-faceted, and often combat adverse trends. Think of your physical immune system. It is strengthened or weakened by many things aside from luck-of-the-draw genetics: where you choose to live, diet, source of foods, nutrition, obtaining needed quantities of certain directly relevant vitamins and minerals, exercise, quantity and quality of sleep, personal relationships, mental attitude, faith, occupation, stress as well as many external factors, such as proximity to or exposure to toxic chemicals. Most trends are disadvantageous, and make it more difficult for you and me to maintain a strong immune system than it was for our grandparents. Our diet consists largely of processed, chemical-laden foods rather than natural foods; our physical environments more congested and polluted; our lives infinitely more complicated, hectic, and stressful. Most of us are not willing to become Amish in order to bolster our immune systems, but we can deliberately influence most of the factors I cited, and we can behave with awareness of how steep the climb, how difficult the task.

I won't belabor the point, but you could engage in the same analysis of the challenges to a healthy emotional immune system.

The same can be said about a business immune system resistant to downward pressures. You need to proactively strengthen it. Doing so involves work on more than one or two things.

CHAPTER 5

How to Compete
with Free

Jason Marrs

Yes, you can compete head-on with free. I do.

When I first met my wife she was getting her Master's Degree in Speech Language Pathology. She was commuting from New York City to Las Cruces, New Mexico as part of a "summers only" program. Basically that meant that she was in school for four months and working for eight. I was an undergrad in marketing who was spending all of my time promoting nightclubs.

She was my first experience with free health care. It was also my first experience helping children with special needs realize their potential. This was something that was at the core of who she was. She had started working with these children as a Special Education Teacher's Aide when she was only 15. From that time, she knew she wanted to work with children and help them communicate. She never believed that she would make money doing this. She felt she would be lucky to just "get by." She became a part of the field because it was her calling. She would do it even if she did not get paid.

She never dreamed that she would become one of the highest paid pediatric Speech Language Pathologists in the country.

That came about a while after we moved back to New York. I had become disgusted and disillusioned working at an advertising agency in New York City so I went to work pushing paper and coordinating therapists for the government contracted agency she was working for. I quickly found myself in a mixture of case management and policy. Dealing with the policy makers, seeing the waste and corruption quickly made me see the dark side of these programs. I saw firsthand that mandates mattered far more than quality. That meant that any therapist with a pulse and a license could get a job. It also meant that children who needed services could not get them because an administrator was kicking the therapist under the table to make sure she didn't recommend "too much." You might call that rationing of care. Get ready.

I saw how favoritism, laziness, vindictiveness, and flat-out corruption was pushing the system further and further into the red, denying patients who legitimately needed care, and driving truly qualified professionals to despair. As you can imagine I was growing progressively more disillusioned with the idea of free.

I told my wife that we had to move into private pay. I saw the risk of staying dependent on the free government system as being too great. While everyone else was saying that these programs were mandated by law I said all it takes is the swipe of a pen and everything changes. Freedom and dependence are mutually exclusive. I knew we had to go. I knew we had to dare to compete with free.

I believed strongly that there was a need for quality services and that people would pay for them. So we set about making that happen. I used my marketing background and she used her pure unadulterated talent. That first year was terrible, really terrible. Money did not come easy. We were hungry. We struggled to make ends meet.

We had not realized that we were up against a system that was entrenched into every nook and cranny of child development. From the time a child is born until they leave home, the professionals they come into contact with are trained to look for the signs that the child may be a candidate for the so-called free programs. There is not a person who works with children in this county, not a preschool, pediatrician, or teacher who does not know about these programs. On top of that the laws are written to favor them and to punish private pay entities like ours. But that was only part of the problem. The other problem was that getting people to pay for something that they thought they could get for free was an enormous challenge.

It took a lot of trial and error to get where we are today. We now have therapists working in our thriving practice commanding fees from $180.00 per hour up to $250.00 per hour. Even when you look at our growing competition in the private pay category most of them fall in the $135.00 to $150.00 range. However, many are down at least as low as $75.00 per hour.

Most business owners are stunned when they learn about my healthcare business and what it is up against. They are also stunned to know that we have been successfully raising our prices during the "great recession." My wife's base services went from $150.00 to $200.00 in 2007, from $200.00 to $220.00 in 2008, and to $250.00 in early 2010. Our other therapists followed a similar path from

> **RESOURCE**
>
> A more detailed, step-by-step plan for selling at a premium even against free is available at www.SimplePricingSystem.com.

SAMPLES OF THE ACTUAL ADVERTISING, MARKETING, AND PRICE
SUPPORT TOOLS JASON USES TO PROMOTE THEIR PRIVATE
PRACTICE APPEAR IN SECTION II OF THIS BOOK.

$160.00 to $200.00 per hour. We've also increased prices on other
services while rapidly increasing demand.

As you can imagine this is something I get asked about a lot
and I am happy to say that I have answers. I do know a thing
or two about getting premium prices even when faced with the
threat of free. As a result I have helped a very diverse range of
businesses deal with this problem.

So What Should You Do?

Obviously before you just jump into competing with free you
need to make sure that is the right thing to do. You want to make
sure you are not fighting a hopeless battle. You want to focus your
resources on wars you can win, not on those that only serve to
drain resources. But assuming that you have done that and have
concluded that you should in fact compete with free I'm going to
give you strategies for succeeding. While different situations call
for different strategies, there are some core strategies that work
in any business. I don't care if you are in health care, lawn care,
info-marketing, photography, luxury travel, or Egyptian monkey
wrestling, these strategies work for everyone.

**The first thing you need to understand is that FREE is not
without cost. Just because there is not a monetary fee does not
mean the customers are not paying something.**

NO B.S. Price Strategy Warning #2

If you fail to help your prospective customers or clients see the "hidden price" of free or cheap, you will always be in a disadvantageous competitive position, because there will almost certainly be others willing to sell or work for far less, or even for free.

Let's take a look at my health care business for an example. If you take the free therapy through the government, you are going to pay by wasting precious time wading through the rivers of red tape to get a therapist of your choosing. If you pay for therapy privately, you can choose the therapist that is best for your child and get started as fast as you want. If you take the free therapy from the government, some bureaucrat, with absolutely no qualifications to do so, will tell you how much therapy you can get. Only when you pay privately are you and your therapist able to do what is in the best interest of your child. When you take the free therapy from the government, your child's history becomes part of his permanent record. When you pay privately, you are in full control of what becomes a part of your child's permanent record. By taking free therapy you pay with wasted time, lost control, uncertain quality, and loss of privacy. Those are not small costs for many people.

You could find similar hidden costs in any product or service being provided for free.

Not long after my son was born we discovered that he had Torticollis—the technical term for a crooked neck. If not corrected through physical therapy it can cause a child to develop incorrectly. It can make them permanently lopsided. Having spent so long in the therapeutic field, my wife knew what it was before she ever sought help.

When she did seek help, the first thing she did was call her contacts to find out who the best person was to work with newborns that have Torticollis. She got the name and moved forward. The physical therapist promptly informed my wife that our son would qualify for free government services. Of course my wife and I already knew that. We also knew that was something we would avoid at all costs. We are fortunate enough to know the value of paying $125.00 per hour for private therapy over taking free therapy from the government. We were also fortunate to have the contacts to find the best therapist for our child.

That brings me to the next point. **It is a myth that any sale is better than no sale.** I know you think you want the broadest market possible. As long as you have that mindset, it will hold you back. It makes your job too hard. You have to get through your head that you are not for everyone. It doesn't matter how many prefer free and won't pay, or even how big the majority want free and won't pay. It only matters there are enough who won't want free—with its costs—and will pay, to support you as you want to be supported. The number of non-buyers and won't-buyers doesn't matter.

There are over six billion people on this planet. There are over three hundred million in the United States. Even in the small little town I grew up in there were 25,000 people. They all have different needs and desires. They all value different things. You cannot attract or serve them all. The vast majority of people will always have zero interest in whatever it is you sell. Your offering may be the center of the universe to you, but it is irrelevant to most people. You must get that through your head.

Even if you were offering everything free, the majority would be disinterested. Even if they did all want what you sell, what would you do if they all tried to buy? You would be seriously screwed. You would not be able to handle it.

So you must determine who really wants what you offer and is willing to pay for it. Who within the population of potential buyers is the most likely to buy what you offer? Who shares your values? Those are your people. Align with them. Give them the things they can't get with the free option. Make no mistake those things do exist. You have to find them and let it be known that you provide them. Once you do that you can attract plenty of buyers who will happily pay a premium for the privilege of doing business with you. If you become very adept at this, as I am in marketing our practice, the law of supply and demand still works to your advantage, even though the overwhelming majority of people are not good prospects for you. But among those who are, who are repelled by the costs of free, and prefer paying for excellence, great demand for you will develop. The more demand you create the more scarce your offering will become in relation to demand and the higher your prices can go as a result. We have been able to raise fees again and again, against the recession, and against both free and low-fee competition, because the demand for us and no one else exceeds our capacity. The best price strategy of all is creating visibly excess demand—in our case, a very busy, thriving practice, often with a waiting list.

The million dollar secret here, summarized, is that every "free" has concealed costs, and when those costs are revealed to a market, there are many customers unwilling to incur the costs of free and profoundly prefer paying for the goods or services they want.

Let's assume you are taking your wife out for dinner at Morton's to celebrate your wedding anniversary, and you are greeted at the door by a frantic manager who explains his busboys have all quit in protest over something, and if you'll put on aprons and bus tables, you can have dinners free at the end of the night. Will you get to work? Probably not. What if he ups the offer to add a free bottle of fine wine to your dinners? Adds a second evening of free dinners and fine wine? At some point I suppose you might be seduced by the free despite its onerous costs, and sacrifice your anniversary celebration. But you ought to consider all the costs. Not just the night as busboy, but however many nights of sleeping on the couch. The kind of customer who frequents Morton's is unlikely to accept these free dinners. Transfer the entire scenario to an Applebee's or a Chili's, and the odds of a customer taking the free go way up. But still, a lot more would decline and go in or go elsewhere and pay money for their celebratory dinner. This is the game played out at airports often, when flights are over-booked. Free roundtrip tickets are offered to anybody who will stay put and wait hours to get on a later flight. If there are 300 on the flight, you never see a stampede of 300 fighting over the free tickets. Sometimes only 2 or 3. Often the airline's announcer has to sweeten the offer, after no takers go to the podium. If it was impossible to combat free, and everybody wanted it, there'd be a mad rush. Why isn't there? Because the majority prefer the cash price they've paid to get where they want to go when they planned on getting there than a free trip now plus another free trip later, with its costs including not getting where they wanted to go when they wanted to get there, waiting around the airport for five boring hours, and uncertainty about really getting out on the next flight. For 295 of 300, the price of free is too high.

Let me summarize the million dollar secret again. Every "free" has concealed costs, and when those costs are revealed to a market, there are many customers who are unwilling to incur the costs of free and who profoundly prefer paying for the goods or services they want.

CHAPTER 6

When FREE Is a Business, Not Just a Price Strategy

Darin Spindler

I n many ways, I share Dan and Jason's deep-seated concerns about the destructive power of Free. I believe it needs to be handled as if petting a porcupine! Yet I am very much in the business of Free, and here to provide a different perspective. One of my businesses, KidsBowlFree.com, has nearly two-million families registered, who participate in its online activities, and are delivered on a silver platter to bowling centers all over North America as potential customers for conversion after their free experience. Yes, I said two-million! With more joining every week. All of which, incidentally, making a number of income streams viable, from advertising and promotion fees paid by brand-name national advertisers as well as local businesses, to the fees paid by the bowling centers.

We are now replicating this business model for diverse small businesses, using www.NewLocalCustomersNow.com, with the intent of managing tens of millions of consumers—leads or prospective customers for businesses, delivered to businesses.

There's a Third, Superior Type of Advertising

Here's an interesting question: would you rather have a sale or a customer? Traditional forms of advertising are all about buying eyeballs and ears, and are typically priced to you, the business owner, based on number of impressions, expressed as circulation, readership, viewership, and sometimes verified by independent auditors, like Nielsen. Some advertisers settle for exposure and hope. Other direct-response advertisers strive for sales. So most advertising is either about brand or a buy-this offer. The first, brand, is then all about hope. You'll remember the brand if and when you feel need or desire for a product or service in its category. A bowling center, for example, would advertise with its name, location, logo, maybe a jingle in a radio spot, and chatter about how much fun bowling can be—and hope. Or a bowling center would focus its advertising on urging people to come in this week and buy two games for the price of one or join a league. This sharply narrows the influence to those very much predisposed to bowling as recreation and ready to spend money doing it. But there's a third option: advertising Free. Done right, Free can broaden appeal and draw in a much larger number of people and get them to try something they would not pay to try. That's a bad thing if there's no good system in place to roll them over from Free to paying, repeat customers, or if the Free is so expansive and openly advertised that it spoils everybody and damages the value of everything you do. It's a very dynamic thing when it's well managed—and for that I have a three-part strategy.

Since you're reading this book, using Free will be counterintuitive, but I'm not talking about doing Free just to do Free, or indiscriminately doing Free either. Instead, there is a three-part strategy you can use involving Free to draw in a lot of good prospective customers, in a controlled way. You need 1) a compelling Free offer that people need to register to get, so you collect their contact information for all the follow-up you care to do; 2) a controlled environment, so the Free offer is directed at the right customers, and there's good reason for it that does not extend to ruining your price positions; 3) a marketing system to convert the people attracted by the Free offer to paying customers immediately after their Free experience. (You can't just let them loose, to wait for the next Free.)

A lot of business owners fear or emotionally dislike Free to such a degree that they unnecessarily pay a lot more to get new customers than they need to. By refusing to "give it away" or by insisting on miserly, nearly free offers, they wind up having to spend a lot more on advertising or promote themselves as cheapest-price providers to attract their customers than if they offered an exceptionally appealing Free. Consider a new restaurant placing a Grand Opening coupon in a Val-Pak mailing delivered to good potential customers in the right neighborhoods, with cost of $500.00. With a very ordinary 2-for-1 offer, they might get 20 customers in the door from 10,000 homes, costing about $25.00 each to get them in the door, less, say $5.00 net on the first tab so each customer costs $20.00. But with an irresistible "Free Dinner for Two, No Strings Attached" offer, they might get 50 customers—reducing cost to $10.00 + $10.00 costs for food = $20.00. Same cost but 2.5 times as many new *prospective* customers. If they used my approach and drove them to a web site to register for the Free Dinner For 2, they might get those same 50 first-time customers in the door immediately, with another 50 or more registered but not immediately showing up, but who could get follow-up marketing. If they made visiting the site much more appealing—maybe with a chance to win some great prizes just for visiting and registering—maybe they could get the same 50 in the door immediately plus 200 for follow-up. If they subsequently convert just 50 of the 200 to come in, they've drawn 100 in for their "free trial," at a cost of just $5.00 each. With a good, immediate conversion process—for example, to a prepaid three-month Dining Club Membership—you can build up a restaurant's business a whole lot faster, with a lot less money tied up in advertising, buying customers for $5.00 rather than for $20.00, and in clumps of 100 rather than in clumps of 20. It's 5 times the number at greater speed but at a quarter of the investment. Wow!

How You Can Do It Too

Just as the above example illustrates, any ordinary business can use Free intelligently, to switch from brand or buy-this-now advertising to lead generation advertising, and to dramatically accelerate growth. Here's exactly how we did this for bowling centers.

Their slowest time is dead of summer. In effect, they have excess, perishable inventory going bad every day in the summer months in the form of capacity not used today, gone forever. We created a program that provides two Free games—entirely free—*every day (!)* all summer to children of certain age. This Free has a price value of over $500.00 per child. It's huge. Parents and kids grasp its value immediately and eagerly snap it up, and it has created a lot of buzz online. Because of the "bigness" of this Free, the bowling centers and KidsBowlFree.com promoting on their behalf do not need to spend a lot of money advertising; it's also viral, and most importantly, it brings a lot of people forward who would otherwise never even think of bowling, let alone buy it. There is an immediate upsell in place, to put some cash in the centers' registers even before anybody shows up to bowl a single game, accomplished online—and, of course, the kids who do come in to bowl free buy sodas and snacks. Because they can come often free, they get addicted, and they rope in all their friends. Because there's logical reason for the Free limited to kids and to summer vacation months only, conversion of these families to paying customers works just fine. Most importantly, we capture every piece of data we need to do very targeted, efficient, and effective follow-up marketing; we successfully get actual addresses, e-mail addresses, phone numbers, and—of enormous subsequent value—birthdays of all the kids and adults in each household before a game is given away.

This "big" Free enabled us to register the first 478,000 families and 1,078,000 kids in just 90 days, entirely online, automatically. Our participating centers are able to spend less on advertising, instead converting their slow season's excess, expiring capacity to capital. With the data collected, we are able to survey and organize these customers throughout the summer, to then conduct precision-targeted marketing campaigns about birthday parties, leagues, and other services. As I was finishing this chapter, we tested a referral campaign, to just 90,000 families in this database and secured 30,000 new customers in 48 hours. We are in the business of managing and mining this continually growing database in as many profitable ways as possible, for the participating centers, for our own company, and for sponsors not competitive with the bowling centers.

With this approach, any business can buy good, convertible leads with Free rather than with advertising dollars. Used this way, carefully, Free becomes a form of capital used to buy an asset, not a "giveaway" that permanently cheapens the business. Obviously, not everybody can do so on the grand scale we are, but don't lose sight of the fact that there are hundreds of bowling centers each using our system. And just about everybody has the needed component parts to replicate this: some slow times or unused capacity that expires if not used, the ability to create a really extraordinary and compelling Free without undermining its other price strategy, and the ability to force registration for the Free through an online data capture place, to create a valuable asset of a well-organized prospect and customer list with a lot of information useful in follow-up and on-going marketing.

Darin Spindler is a marketing consultant and specialist in lead generation and online marketing for independent and franchised brick-and-mortar local businesses. His systems have created well over five-million new customers for local business owners coast to coast. Types of businesses now participating in Darin's nationwide new customer development programs go far beyond the original bowling centers to include restaurants and taverns, movie theaters, golf courses, learning centers, hair salons, tanning salons, health clubs and fitness centers, health care practices, home remodeling contractors, dry cleaners, and over 50 other categories. He works closely with Dan Kennedy in the development and operation of "done-for-them" lead generation marketing systems for these businesses. Complete information and, of course, a compelling Free can be found at: www.NewLocalCustomersNow.com/Kennedy.

CHAPTER 7

Antidotes to
Commodity Thinking

Jason Marrs

Few business owners begin with the goal of being average. They hope for more. Yet most permit themselves to be boxed in to average by their prices, led by thinking of their products or services as ordinary commodities. If what you deliver isn't truly unique and special, how can you charge anything but ordinary and average prices? This acceptance of commodity thinking is everywhere—and it drives me insane!

The sad thing about it is that every business that is selling a commodity is doing so by choice. And they'll continue to sell commodities, think of themselves as selling commodities, and being commoditized, until they make the decision not to. **The minute you decide not to think of whatever you sell as a commodity, you liberate new, different, and better price possibilities.**

Commodities

For purposes of this discussion, a COMMODITY is an ordinary, common, even mundane product or service that, in the absence of differentiation deliberately created by its provider, is perceived by consumers as having limited, usually low value, and being interchangeable with other products or services of its type. Generally speaking, for consumers, grocery items, household cleaners, paper products, batteries, gasoline, auto insurance, and a car wash are commodities. For business/industry things like raw materials, cleaning supplies, office supplies are commodities. A universal example would be coffee. To a great many consumers, coffee is coffee and there is no reason to pay more for one brand or another, or to favor getting it from the convenience store on the far side vs. the near side of the street. If anything, lowest price might sway such a decision. Yet Dunkin' Donuts and Starbucks prosper, at successively higher price levels. Aspirin is, *in fact*, aspirin, yet Bayer Apirin exsists as a brand and sells for a higher price than the generic equivalent, side-by-side on the same shelf. Permitting yourself to be perceived as an interchangeable commodity, i.e., commoditized is a fast and certain path to price and profit erosion.

There is no such thing as a commodity, there is only commodity thinking. To prove it, let me ask you a question: *Can you get more commoditized than air?* No, you can't. Oxygen is the most abundant element on earth. It makes up 90% of water. You can't take a breath on this planet without it. It is free to everyone. No need to buy it. You'd think that it could not be sold, but it is. And I'm not talking about oxygen tanks for the sick. I'm talking about oxygen being sold to healthy people. One place this occurs is in "oxygen bars." The FDA argues that it's not healthy to breath pure oxygen and that oxygen bars are breaking the law. However, that doesn't stop people from selling oxygen to the public. Oxygen bars, spas, and other trendy places are selling oxygen for as much as $1.00 per minute. You can even get it in various scents and flavors, like strawberry oxygen. But any way you look at it, you are paying $60.00 an hour just to breathe.

Does that seem outrageous? Brace yourself. $60.00 an hour is a steal when you compare it to what www.go2air.com is doing. They sell Personal Oxygen Devices for $19.99 each. What do you get for your money? You get roughly forty breaths. Considering the average human takes roughly 15 breaths per minute you're getting 2.7 minutes. That translates to $7.40 per minute to breath.

FIGURE 7.1: Website page from www.go2air.com.
Reprinted with Permission.

That's a staggering $444.22 per hour. Of course, this is being sold as a health product. But it's air.

If you accept the idea that these guys are helping people improve their health, you might then insist that you don't do anything that important or beneficial. Or that devices providing pure oxygen are unique despite their dispensing the most readily available, free commodity there is. Well, in that case let's take a look at something you cannot possibly make that argument about: underwear.

We can all agree that underwear qualifies as a commodity. Most people wear it. Women can buy a six-pack of Hanes for around $1.33 a pair, so they don't *need* to pay $5.00 or more a pair for Victoria's Secret. But they do. That may not sound like a lot in terms of dollars but it is a 300% price difference. But why stop at a paltry 300% increase? The Australian Wicked Weasel brand has an entry-level Hipster Cotton Workwear for $15.42 each. That puts their panty well over 1,000% higher priced than the Hanes panty and roughly 300% higher priced than the Victoria's Secret panty. All three are cotton bikini panties. Not much difference in the actual panty but a huge discrepancy in prices.

Even if you combine all of their prices together they still pale in comparison to the price of our next example. If you go to www.NancyMeyer.com you can buy the Carine Gilson Silk & Lace Shorty for the everyday low price of $448.00. Admittedly it's not cotton like the others, but it isn't spun gold either. It has no jewels. It is just a lace panty (Figure 7.2). That sure is a long ways from $1.33 isn't it?

I recently had a long, drawn-out conversation with a lady who was the owner of what she considered to be an upscale lingerie boutique. I mentioned something about the Carine Gilson panty and she said, "I don't know of any pants that are that expensive." I said no, not pants—*panties*. She kept hearing pants. She could not imagine pants, let alone panties costing

FIGURE 7.2: Website page from www.NancyMeyer.com.
Reprinted with Permission.

that much money. She flatly refused to believe that I was saying panty. She had been in the business for 35 years and "knew" such a thing was not possible.

Not only are such prices possible, they are not even rare. There are super exclusive "jeweled" panties that can go for millions of dollars that are rare. I didn't include them just because they are too easy for someone to write off as an anomaly. The ones I included are not. They are something that anyone with the money can buy. You do not need special connections. You can buy any one of them right now if you have the money. Many, many, many women do. Everyday. Some, routinely.

The woman who owned her own lingerie store was also wrong about the existence of $450.00 jeans. They are not considered expensive in many circles. $450.00 is actually the base price of many luxury brands. In fact, that price is but a tiny fraction of the $4,000.00 starting price tag attached to a pair of APO Jeans of New York with diamond buttons and rivets. See Figure 7.3.

FIGURE 7.3: Website page from www.apojeans.com.
Reprinted with Permission.

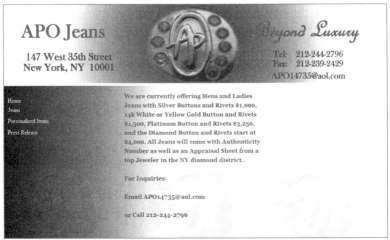

Each of these things has a focus on individuality and how it makes you feel. It may not be explicitly said, but it is there. That sense of individuality is what drives such purchases. You don't spend $4,000.00 on pants for function. You do it to make a statement to yourself and those around you. Personally I appreciate the audacity of those who create them. They are doing the necessary task of moving money around and pushing us forward. It does not matter if the majority appreciates it or even understands it. It is essential that they not be deterred.

One final, mind-expanding example: Kopi Luwak. That's a fancy name for cat-poo coffee. The Asian Civit Cat, which is actually more like a weasel than a cat, has a fondness for coffee beans (Figure 7.4). They are said to eat only the best berries from the coffee plant. These beans then pass through the cat's digestive tract mostly un-digested. Workers then search the jungle collecting cat-poo that gets turned into the world's most expensive coffee. (Think about this the next time you're walking your dog with baggie in hand or are out in your own yard with

FIGURE 7.4: Website page from www.bantaicivitcoffee.com.

Reprinted with Permission.

a pooper-scooper. If only that pup ate coffee beans, you could be rich!) At www.bantaicivitcoffee.com the cat-poop coffee sells for $85.00 per 4oz bag. Or you can save $20.00 by buying a pound for $320.00.

I'm curious about the taste, but I just haven't been able to talk myself into consuming something that's from a cat's butt. My views don't matter. Neither do yours. That gets us back to the larger point here. While you must believe in what you sell, your opinion is not nearly as important as that of your buyers. They are the ones who decide what is worth their money or not. The world would be an awfully mundane place if we all liked the same things. It is your job to align your offering with a group of people who love what you are selling and are willing to pay for it.

Don't tell me that you can't alter the perception of any commodity. I've just demonstrated it with air, underwear, and coffee—coffee made from cat crap no less! When it comes to price, "can't" is a symptom of commodity thinking, not a reality. You need to change the word to "won't." The reality is that any commodity can be differentiated and sold for a premium price. All it takes is the willingness to do it and a pricing strategy to make it happen.

How To Conquer the #1 Enemy of Maximum Profitability: Commoditization

I have a little history lesson, and journey forward in retail, for you—as motivation to resist with all your might commoditization and the price strategy it compels.

In the late 1800s there was a common scam in which manufacturers and wholesalers would send merchandise to retailers who had not ordered it. If the retailer refused to take the shipment the wholesaler would reduce the price in order to make the sale. The wholesaler would apologize for the "mistake" and, in order to save the cost of return freight, offer to let the retailer keep it for a much lower price than shown on the invoice packed in with the goods. Oftentimes this tactic worked. Other times it did not. This same sneaky ploy is still used today, by the way.

One such attempt occurred between a watch manufacturer and its intended bamboozled buyer, a retail shop owner named Edward Stegerson. You've undoubtedly never heard of Ed. Yet his obstinate decision to refuse a shipment of gold watches created something very big in American history. A 22-year-old railroad station agent caught in the middle of the dispute made an agreement with the watchmaker to keep and sell the watches on consignment, and keep any profit he made beyond $12.00 per watch. The young man was so happy with the outcome he promptly ordered another shipment of watches and began to sell them through mail-order catalogs. This led him into the mail-order business. It wasn't long before he moved to Chicago and met another man who would become his first employee. In 1893, these fellows created the Sears & Roebuck Company. Maybe you've heard of it?

The company was based on the premise that people will buy if you give them quality goods and low prices. Their original catalog was proudly titled "The Great Price Maker." They were selling against local stores and able to undercut their prices, in exactly the same way that today's e-commerce variety retailers like amazon.com and overstock.com do. In 1925, they opened their first retail store and went on to become America's largest retailer. Today, some online merchants have also opened brick-and-mortar stores.

The future did not stay bright for Sears forever. It was not the only company to have the bright idea of selling more volume for less profit. Aside from five-and-dimes such as F.W. Woolworth Company, other companies such as Kmart and Walmart emerged as did the "category killers" starting with Toys 'R Us. Category killers got their name because of their propensity for dominating a specific category. Toys 'R Us, Office Max, 84 Lumber, Circuit City, Barnes & Noble are but a few of the names who came into categories and choked out the competition with advanced strategies for driving prices lower. Many of these became vulnerable in time. The hazards of change very much affect retail as well as direct marketing, and a lot of vulnerability is tied to price strategy. Customer loyalty is difficult to develop and maintain under any circumstance, but the difficulty is only magnified when you compete primarily on price. Once you start to compete on price then you can count on there being somebody coming along who'll beat your prices, even if doing so ultimately bankrupts them. There is no glory in having the second lowest price. When you compete on price you have no choice but to be the cheapest. Second cheapest is not good enough. As a result, price wars are fought constantly and the race to the bottom continues to intensify while the margin for error continues to shrink.

This battlefield is littered with casualties. F.W. Woolworth Company is gone. 84 Lumber has been squeezed out by Home Depot. Circuit City went bankrupt. Barnes & Noble now stands in the shadow of Amazon.com. Office Max finds itself being squeezed out by Staples who is being squeezed by Costco and Sam's Club. The original giant Sears has been bought out by Kmart. That has done little to help Kmart compete with the 3,000-pound gorilla, Walmart who squeezes just about everybody.

But Walmart dare not feel too smug. It now finds itself being squeezed by Amazon.com on just about every front. Not content with just being the world's largest bookstore, Amazon has moved into selling just about everything under the sun. They also have mind-numbing technological expertise and a use of logistics that clearly rivals Walmart's. Another competitive advantage Amazon has is not being bogged down with the upkeep of brick-and-mortar facilities. More importantly, they have never been burdened with the task of getting their customers out of their house and into the store. Amazon's buyers have always been trained to buy from them while sitting at a computer. Now that smart phones have evolved, Amazon's buyers are able to access them from anywhere. When you combine that with their free shipping options, you have an extremely powerful force. Now, anytime you are shopping you can compare the price in whatever store you're standing in with Amazon via your smart phone. Uh-oh. Make no mistake; Amazon is the rising giant *in the discount category.* However, it is not safe from threats. Amazon may come to dominate the retail landscape, but they will not hold that position based on price forever. No one ever has. No one ever will. A competitive advantage of a low price cannot be maintained forever. It is an unsustainable advantage. Keep that in mind whenever you head in this direction.

Just Because You Can Does Not Mean You Should

In 1993 there was a blockbuster movie called Jurassic Park. It was about a billionaire who used a new genetic technology to bring dinosaurs to life in the present. His plan was to make a theme park in which tourists would be taken on safari to see the impossible: all of these extinct, prehistoric beasts come back to life. He ran into a "little" problem that greatly concerned his investors, so he brought in some scientists to help calm their nerves. He believed if he could win over the scientists he could win over his investors. One of the scientists was a chaos theorist named Dr. Ian Malcolm who was played by Jeff Goldblum. Dr. Malcolm made a point that everyone who got so excited by what they *could* do never stopped to ask if they *should* do it. That is something any purveyors of cheap or free, as well as any marketers allowing themselves to be classified as a purveyor of commodities need to ask themselves. Even if you can—temporarily—win a price war, should you? Even if you can make good money—temporarily—selling goods or services thought of by you and your customers as commodities, should you? At Jurassic Park, it turned out that the problem with those reincarnated monsters wasn't very manageable. The beasts insisted on eating the tourists.

While many business leaders have been busily racing to the price bottom, they have sacrificed the quality of their offerings, their position and relationship with their customers, shareholders' wealth, and employees' jobs. They are also driving the throw-away society, trying to price in a way people are accepting of short-lived quality. The founder of Toys 'R Us, Charles Lazarus, said that he left the baby furniture business and went into toys because baby furniture doesn't wear out and toys do. Of course, IKEA proved that wrong. IKEA led the way in making furniture disposable. Today it seems like most furniture is disposable. Walk into homes all across America and you'll

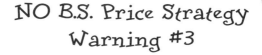

NO B.S. Price Strategy Warning #3

The bargain of a cheap price and securing of a big discount may satisfy a customer momentarily, but only real value, quality, and service can retain that customer. If you sacrifice the latter for the former, be prepared to endlessly chase and always, desperately need more new customers that you pour into a bucket with a hole in the bottom as big as the hole at the top.

find furniture that looks good but cannot stand up to moderate, let alone heavy, use. Other than Styrofoam, nothing you or I buy from a discounter is going to last for any prolonged amount of time. Junk currently litters the landscape, *inside* homes and offices.

Brand names are also deteriorating. There was a time when a name-brand meant something. Now its meaning is highly place dependent. Many of the big boxes force their suppliers to make their products to their specifications. This is just, then, a case of paying for the label. A similar thing is happening with retail outlets. There was a time when you went to the outlet stores to buy something of top quality from a famous, respected brand, that had some little unintentional imperfection, or was out of season, or manufactured to point of overstock. Now you go to the outlet and buy something intentionally made inferior by the company. The only thing that is the same is the label. Products sold in the outlet stores are made specifically for the outlet stores. Same with outlet stores online. Obviously, this *can* be done—it is being done. But *should* it be done?

American business, from big migrating down to small, has increasingly focused on shorter-, shorter-, and shorter-term results, with leadership willing to take profits today at certain, serious expense, risk, and damage in the long term. You have to weigh that carefully. If you intend to have your shops, stores, restaurants, service businesses and practices prosper in your community for your entire life, then the price strategy embraced by some Fortune 500 CEOs captive to Wall Street, obsessed with quarterly earnings numbers and willing to do his five years, grab his golden parachute, and bail out, leaving the mess for the next guy may not be the best price strategy for you!

Discounters Happy Being Commoditized Are Not All Bad

You would think that as strongly as I argue against this approach to business—accepting me-too, me-same commoditization and relying on discounting—I would not have *anything* good to say about discounters. That would be wrong; I do. This type of business does serve a useful purpose. They are a necessary component of competition. We need businesses who seek to make offerings cheaper so that more and more people can afford them, so that goods are available to all regardless of their incomes, and as a motivational force for the rest of us to be more creative about product, service, positioning, and price strategy.

However, presently, far too many businesses are spending all of their time and energy trying to cut costs so that they can be the cheapest. Not nearly enough of them are spending time trying to figure out how to increase quality so they can spend more and be the best. The near-collapse of the economy in 2008, and the recession dragging on since, has many abandoning their successful strategies in favor of slashing every possible cost despite severe damage to service and quality, then reputation. The pyramid has gotten very, very broad and crowded toward the bottom. This has created great opportunity toward the top for those courageous and creative marketers who take notice.

The Secret of the Living

Trying to compete with the big chain stores is so scary that during the early part of the last century the federal government passed laws such as the Clayton Act of 1914 and the Robison-Patman Act of 1936 to restrict discounters' ability to use price as a weapon. The big retailers were seen as anti-competitive and a threat to independent mom-and-pop shops. Never mind that the legislation actually did more to hamper competition than it did to promote it. The fact remains that almost one hundred years later the big chains with their ability to commoditize everything has not killed us yet. The weak or weakened, frightened, lazy, and uncreative in any industry often turn to government for protection by regulation from tougher competitors, but even when it is given, it fails to provide sustained safe shelter, and generally has unintended negative consequences for both business and consumers. Giants cut down to size and caged break free and return to the fight, enraged.

I am unaware of a type of product that is not offered by giant discounters who act as a commoditizing force. They cover everything from groceries, to electronics, home goods, health supplies, health care, building materials, toys, books, even, ironically, luxury goods. There are chain restaurants that commoditize dining out. To take that a step further, there are even companies that are commoditizing dinner at home. Grocery stores now carry just about any pre-prepared dinner you can get at a restaurant. They even cover many services. There are companies that have commoditized advertising, marketing, printing, publishing, even legal services. I used LegalZoom.com the last time I set up one of my corporations. They also did wills for my wife and me. It was a simple process. There is very little you can do to escape the reach of commoditization or discounting.

All this commoditization has been horribly disruptive, intimidating, and confusing, and has killed many mom-and-pop shops; but for every business killed by it, many survive, and some even thrive. **Why isn't the impact of commoditization universal? Why doesn't discounting force everyone in the category to discount? How can there be a price war with conscientious objectors who prosper? The answer is a big glaring secret hidden in plain sight: some people are willing to knowingly pay more**.

The profitable question for you is: *why?*

I watched with interest as a local model train store in my community wrestled with this same question. He was terrified when Walmart came to town and said he'd never be able to survive against the giant. I challenged him, and told him there could be more opportunity for him in the giant's shadow than in the open sunlight BW (Before Walmart). Four years later, he is thriving and, as I predicted, doing even better than he was before. How? By capitalizing from the increased traffic. He isn't even doing anything particularly impressive with his marketing. In his case, he simply does not provide a single thing that can be found at Walmart. Instead, he focuses on highly specialized products for serious hobbyists, for nostalgia-driven toy buyers emotionally connected to products where price doesn't matter, and on service. He came to understand and profit from the same kinds of reasons women spend a multiple of what they'd pay at Walmart to buy cotton panties from Victoria's Secret. The reason I bought my son a $20.00 handmade wooden baby rattle and why every year I order my daughter's Halloween costume from Chasing Fireflies, when I could find rattles and costumes for less at Walmart. You do it with something, too. No, you do it with many things. There is always a lower-cost, commoditized version of whatever it is you are buying. Why don't *you* always buy the cheapest commodity?

Everyone defaulting to cheaper or cheapest price strategy and agreeing to participate in commodity merchandising is always in the process of dying by suicide. Some faster than others, some almost imperceptibly for a long time then suddenly speeding up. Everyone refusing this death is living.

Yes, Everybody in Marketing Points to Starbucks . . .

There are countless examples of companies thriving while selling what could be considered a commodity. The one most often given is Starbucks. Ironically, it has become something of a commodity in and of itself. There is a Starbucks on every corner. There are Starbucks products in groceries. Even, most recently, Starbucks instant coffee. It seems to me that they've given in to temporary profit strategies that are slowly eating away at their brand value, like unseen termites destroying a house from the inside out. Time will tell. But they may be on a death march. My co-author is a fan of Howard Schultz, Starbucks' founder, celebrated his return to reinvigorate the spirit of a troubled company, owns stock in the company, is happy with his returns, and cautiously optimistic about the company's future—but he admits his best ideas seem to be in the past. There you can find a number of anti-commoditization lessons. Schultz' book about the company's beginnings, *Pour Your Heart Into It: How Starbucks Built a Company One Cup at a Time,* is well worth reading.

My favorite company that is *currently* defying commoditization is The Republic of Tea. As you might have guessed, they sell tea. *Tea.* They call themselves the leading purveyor of premium teas. While you can pick up a box of 100 Lipton teabags for around $5.00 you will need to shell out over $20.00 for the same size box from The Republic of Tea. That is by no means close to their most expensive tea. They sell a rare Darjeeling for over $16.00 per ounce. They are very much positioning their tea away from other caffeinated beverages and alongside fine wines. In fact, when you buy bottled tea from them it comes in a tall fancy bottle, has tasting notes, and recommended dishes to help you pair the tea correctly.

The Republic of Tea is a storytelling company. Their marketing is both educational and fanciful. Like Disney, everyone has a clever name. Customers are "Citizens" and the people in the company are "Ministers" and "Ambassadors." They have the Minister of Leaves, The Prime Minister, and The Minister of Distribution to name a few. The Republic of Tea is selling a concept—not a commodity. They have moved far beyond tea to selling a lifestyle. They make drinking tea a fun and engaging experience even though you are drinking it in your own home and not in their shop. To sell at four times the price of their commoditized competition they had better do something special, and they do. So, the price of tea bags or bottled tea at Walmart is of no significance to them.

The Dynamic Power of Radical Individualism

I have not personally set foot in a Walmart in years. Dan Kennedy says I should, from time to time, to keep tabs on what they're up to, and he's right, so should you. But I can't bring myself to buy anything there. I hate the lines. I hate the ambiance. It is a painful experience to me. In fact the last time I went there I actually split my head open. I stepped around a corner into a metal post that was sticking out. It cut a "V" into the middle of my forehead. Maybe unfairly, the impression left in my mind after the cut and bruise healed is that providing dirt-cheap prices is more important to them than even their customers' safety. It may have low prices, but it is just not my kind of place.

I'm not alone in that sentiment. Some people just don't like the store. Sometimes it is for reasons like mine. For others, it's a moral issue. They don't like what it stands for. This sentiment is not unique to Walmart. It is growing for all of the big mass merchandise companies. Many people are looking beyond the low sticker prices and seeing the other costs, economic and societal. Another factor is what a March 2010 Ogilvy and Mather survey called the "emergence of radical individualism." More and more consumers, 73% according to their study, would rather have fewer, high-quality things, than buy the most bulk they can for each buck. Better a home very nicely appointed than filled with as much stuff as can be bought at lowest prices and piled high in every room. This is part of a movement towards more sustainable living, whether it is environmental or financial. I believe it a hallmark of what Dan Kennedy speaks of as the emerging New Economy. People are getting weary of being throw-away consumers. Some are influenced in this by the green movement and concern for the environment. For more, the economic chaos and trauma we've encountered in recent years is fueling this sentiment. The desire to at least feel more financially responsible and prudent is with many almost to the extent it existed post-Depression, and, rather than encouraging buying cheap goods at cheapest prices, it is instead inspiring seeking better products. Many local communities are also re-embracing Main Street merchants and locally-based companies.

All this plays to the power of radical individualism. It's the newest consumer revolution. Rejection of mass merchandise and mass merchandisers, desire for something more special if not unique, personal, is what really matters. This gives you, the marketer, the perfect opportunity to step forward and stand out, and call out to these revolutionist customers.

When Higher Prices Sell More

Dan Kennedy

There is an ad in my archives, in which this tag-line appears:

REASSURINGLY EXPENSIVE.

It doesn't matter what product was advertised this way—wine, snow tires, my professional services. Any number of things could be advertised this way, and many should, because there are many cases of more volume of sales achieved by raising prices.

In a price test of $97.00 versus $127.00 per year for a B2B news-letter, conventional wisdom says crossing the hundred dollar line should suppress response. But, in this actual case, the $127.00 price pulled 11% higher response.* Did the higher price cause prospects to think the newsletter much more valuable? The higher response combined with the 31% higher price produces 45% more revenue, a major victory. Another case: a book originally priced at $24.95 sold just as well at three payments of $8.99 ($26.95 total, $2.00 more revenue per sale). Point: higher prices do not necessarily mean poorer response. Point: you can't know if you don't test, and re-test frequently. *(*Source: article by Mark Everett Johnson, targetmarketingmag.com).*

Warning: The tendency in tough times is to cut prices, without any empirical evidence that doing so increases profits, and without carefully calculating impact on net profit. Sacrificing margin for volume, even preservation of volume, can be a losing proposition; a dangerous, slippery slope. A good question posed in Mark's article: do you need to cut prices to win more orders from tight-fisted customers or do you need to raise prices to keep up with rising costs? The second part of that question begs consideration of a Truth's application, in your business; there are certain customers who will buy certain things regardless of price (or price increase). If you offer such a thing to such a group of customers, *all* price-cutting does is trade away margin.

One reason that a higher price may move more goods is that it is perceived as the more appropriate price by the customers. If you got a direct-mail piece in your mail offering nearly new, fully reconditioned and warranteed Rolex® watches for $49.95, how would you react? Even if from a local jewelry store of good reputation, you would be very skeptical. Many would never go into the store, presuming the offer was a scam, to lure people in for some sort of bait-and-switch. If you did go in, you'd be very wary and anxious. Obviously, $49.95 is a completely inappropriate price for a Rolex®, and even I would be hard-pressed to think of a reason-why story that could reassure people that they really were getting a good Rolex® at that price. So, add a zero. $499.50. Now what? Some people only vaguely familiar with the Rolex® brand might be lured. But most would still be repelled. If price was communicated as "from $1,499.50 to $4,999.50," many more might be brought in, bargain-hunting within a realm of prices they viewed as possible, especially if a good reason why is given in the advertisement. Selling Rolex® watches for $400.00 would be a much more difficult task than selling them for $4,000.00.

In the back of every intelligent customer's mind is the oft-repeated warning: if it sounds too good to be true, it is. This can be overridden even with sophisticated buyers by a combination of extreme benefit—such as extraordinary investment returns, triggering greed to trump common sense. Think of the Bernie Madoff story. But, usually, many other reassurances are also needed, such as, in his case, referrals from trusted friends within the same circles, his exalted reputation including having served in an advisory capacity with the New York Stock Exchange, and a complex mythology built and carefully maintained, including active, visible philanthropy. And you don't want to run a fraudulent scheme anyway, do you? Ironically, it can be easier to commit fraud than to persuade people of the value of the legitimate. Because you are unlikely to offer such extreme benefit and trigger such powerful emotions, you need to reassure your buyers more thoroughly. Price can be reassuring or anxiety and skepticism producing.

CHAPTER 8

The Power of Preeminence
as Price Strategy

Dr. Barry Lycka

I imagine every business owner or professional longs for *one simple thing* they can do to be paid what they are really worth, without haggling, negotiating or endless discounting, and to develop a secure business with enough profit to sustain itself. I have done that, under difficult conditions, but not, I'm afraid, with one simple thing. Unless you'd like to classify "marketplace dominance" as a simple thing.

I operate an independent cosmetic surgery-medical practice in Edmonton, Alberta, Canada, up against government interference and managed care controls more draconian and overwhelming than everything doctors in the U.S. may face under Obamacare. Here, fees are strictly regulated for all services so that every doctor is supposedly on equal footing. It is even illegal to bill for something outside the controls of this health care system, if there is a procedure intended to address the need covered by the health care system, regardless of the doctor's judgments about what may be best for the patient.

Unlike most doctors who surrender and suffer, in 1991, I decided to opt out of the system entirely, totally control my own destiny, and build a fee-for-service, cash-only cosmetic practice. This was something virtually unheard of at the time. I knew I would have to be a dominating presence in my niche and in my market just to survive. My problem wasn't just price, as is discussed throughout this book, but asking patients to pay my prices with their own cash rather than with government health care or insurance forms and their signatures. I'll quickly say, if I can achieve this here, in Canada, it can be done anywhere. Today, I have dozens of U.S. doctors with varied kinds of practices in my coaching/mastermind groups where, together, we work on independence strategies. I'm proud to be something of a Moses, leading my people to a better place!

Anyway, back in 1991, I made a strategic and daring decision to navigate regulatory and consumer resistance, and transition from a traditional dermatology practice to one specializing in certain types of cosmetic surgery. Over about four years, I experimented with different price strategies, different promotional approaches, discarding many and keeping and building on a few. In the process, two different Canadian regulatory agencies attacked, and I battled one to a draw, the other to a reversal of its rulings in court.

All along, I knew that there were certain patients hidden among the masses, who would actually prefer the ultimate level of personal attention and care, the most advanced procedures and technology, and would be more than willing to pay top fees to get it. I think this is an important foundation for all other ideas in this book; that hidden among the masses, there are customers, clients, or patients who are a perfect match with whatever the best is, that you can deliver, and who will be happy to choose you over all other alternatives—including lower-priced ones. I took two approaches to attracting these kinds of patients for my practice.

Approach One:
The Hawaiian Fisherman's Method

One year, on vacation in Hawaii, I was relaxing at a beach, watching whales in the distance, when a fisherman, obviously a local, drove up in his pick-up truck. He got out with a dozen fishing rods. Not one. A dozen. He baited each hook, cast all the lines into the ocean, and set the rods in the sand. Intrigued, I wandered over and asked him for an explanation.

"It's simple," he said. "I love fish but I hate fishin'. I like eatin', not catchn'. So I cast out 12 lines. By sunset, some of them will have caught a fish. Never all of 'em. So if I only cast one or two I might go hungry. But 12 is enough so some always catch. Usually there's enough for me and extras to sell to local restaurants. This way, I live the life I want."

The simple fellow had unwittingly put his finger on a powerful secret. The flaw in most businesses, that keeps them always in desperate need—which suppresses prices—is: too few lines cast in the ocean. The best way for me to be sure that I always had at least a new patient arriving of the right mindset and financial capability to qualify for my practice was to cast a lot of lines in the ocean everyday. A lot of lines at sunrise, never hungry at sunset.

The results have been superlative. I have developed a practice income of millions of dollars annually, but that still does not require all of my time, so that I can develop the nonprofit Canadian Skin Cancer Foundation; develop my online portal, WellAndWiseOnline.com, a consumer/patient education site; run my coaching/mastermind groups for physicians; and spend time with my wife of 25 years, four grown children and grandchildren—and take those vacations. At age 56, I could retire if I wanted to. I make my work life easier every way I can, such as flying to conferences and speaking engagements by private jet. All this created against stiff headwinds of an autonomy-unfriendly regulatory environment and a jaded marketplace unaccustomed to paying top dollar for any health care.

Approach Two:
The Triangle of Pre-Eminence

Dan Kennedy and another celebrated thought-leader in marketing and business development, his friend Jay Abraham, both speak of the power of preeminence. Preeminence means "surpassing all others in a distinguished way." That was the second thing I set out to do. In attacking this objective, I developed what I now teach as the Triangle of Preeminence: expertise and excellence in patient/customer service; extraordinarily effective, high-visibility marketing; and generosity in community service and involvement. With this Triangle, any professional or business owner can stand out so dramatically from any crowd, that he will attract patients/clients of the attitude and philosophy that price is the least of their concerns!

If you were to visit my practice, you would find a state-of-the-art facility, first-class environment, and personable, caring, well-educated staff. I have been doing my signature procedure—liposuction—since 1986, and as every new advancement has occurred, I've evaluated it, studied it, if appropriate, taken special training in it, and invested in the finest technology. This has partly liberated me from getting all my patients locally;

in fact, patients come for my "Ultimate Liposuction" from the United States, Europe, South America, and Asia. In the area of wrinkle-erasing treatments, I don't just inject Botox® like many doctors—I combine a number of anti-aging and skin treatments into my own proprietary procedure, making price comparison impossible. This is all part of the first side of the triangle: expertise and excellent service. Another way to say it is *incomparable* expertise and service, deliberately designed and presented so it cannot be compared.

If you were to spend any time in Edmonton, you would encounter my high-profile marketing. I use television, radio, newspapers, and the internet on an almost daily basis. I also pride myself in "event marketing." Several times a year, I create seminars, open-house events, guest-celebrity events. Each is carefully planned, each is preceded by weeks of multi-media saturation advertising and publicity, each is attended by hundreds of new patients, and each is usually covered favorably by the local press. I invest to be sure there is no question who is THE leading authority on and provider of these procedures in my area. It's important to recognize that this level of use of media requires a premium price strategy with sufficient, above-par profit built in.

Finally, as the third leg of the triangle, I often tie my events to local charities and organizations, I lend other support to local causes, and am visibly developing the Canadian Skin Cancer Foundation with the ambitious goal of eradicating skin cancer from the planet! I also contribute to the literature and thought-leadership of my profession, and am the author of the book *Shaping a New Image: The Practice of Cosmetic Surgery* (CJSM Publishing, 2001), a speaker at professional conferences, and as already mentioned, a coach and mentor to other doctors. Taking activist and leadership roles in your community and in your industry or profession is a good opportunity to contribute while also elevating your status and creating additional reassurance of exceptional expertise for your patients/customers.

When I talk with the doctors I coach about fees/prices—and you can rest assured, the subject often comes up!—I tell them that it's a mistake to take it out of context and think about it in isolation, as a separate matter. Price is interwoven with many other factors, including The Triangle and the Hawaiian fisherman's method discussed here.

Dr. Barry A.S. Lycka, M.D., FRCPC is a prominent physician, lecturer, and business consultant and mentor to other physicians worldwide, including those participating in his private coaching/ mastermind groups. **Information for doctors and other business owners is available at www. aestheticprofits.com/mastermind; for everyone at www.WellAndWiseOnline.com.** Dr. Lycka can be reached at www.BarryLyckaMD.com. He is also a contributor to several other Dan Kennedy books, including *Uncensored Sales Strategies* by Sydney Biddle Barrows and Dan Kennedy; *No B.S. Marketing to the Affluent*; and *The Ultimate Marketing Plan*.

CHAPTER 9

B2B Price Wars and
The Way of the
Warriors Who Win

Dan Kennedy

Most B2B marketers succumb to the idea of competition-driven pricing. By accepting this as a fact of life, they surrender in advance and preclude other possibilities. Real warriors, of course, are disgusted by the idea of surrender, so they gravitate to the other choice: controlling the competitive environment via superior, category of one positioning, more effective marketing, and unique value propositions. In short, differentiation. When I explain this and get a stubborn business owner insisting he is in a commoditized category and has no differentiation to offer, I tell him to slit his wrists and get it over with. After all, if the brain is already dead, why keep the body alive?

Some years back, I was speaking at the national convention of the Advertising Specialty Institute and encountered a spectacularly obtuse company owner. ASI's population is comprised of all the companies that sell imprinted ballpoint pens, baseball caps, coffee mugs, and every other sort of promotional product. At the time, the internet was just beginning to exert real influence, and many—maybe most—in this field felt terrorized by price shopping made mouse-click easy. I began my speech by saying: if you believe you are in a commodities business, get out. This woman took me *very* literally. She stormed out of the room. Later, she sent her complaint letter to all parties concerned, accusing me of being ill-informed, ill-prepared, and vile, because, of course, they all *were* in a commodity business. But her facts and mine differed. No one in the promotional products and ad specialty industry needs be in a commodity business unless they choose to, but they don't need to exit their industry either.

Keith and Travis Lee, owners of 3-D (for 3-Dimensional) Mailings, Inc.—who contribute their own price strategy elsewhere in this book—are great examples. They sell all those products, but they specialize in selling them for use in clever direct-mail campaigns, with the copy, graphics, offer, and theme of the mailing matched to the imprinted doohickey, and they work with the client to devise the entire campaign. You can see their approach to this business at 3DMailResults.com. Yes, you can buy most of the doodads they sell other places, but you can't buy their expertise. Further, they focus on reaching clients in clumps, as vendor-partners of marketing gurus, trainers, consultants, and coaches like me and many in different niches, from dentistry to financial planning to lawn care. They match their theme campaigns and doodads to the strategies the gurus teach, and are brought to the guru's clientele as a resource. The combination of these two positioning and marketing strategies permits the best price strategy of all: ignoring all price competition. Ironically, this has made their business so successful they can buy in big volume and buy direct from overseas manufacturers, so, often, they now also have the lowest prices. Another in the industry, who I've also coached in business as I have Keith and Travis, is B. Shawn Warren. He sells the same kind of imprinted items as part of his business, but he has specialized in serving fraternal organizations like Kiwanis, the Elks, veterans groups, and civic clubs. Another, a company called SmartPractice, created by my friends Jim and Naomi Rhode, specializes only in the dental, chiropractic, and medical fields. Their products might be commodities, but they have made sure their businesses transcend commoditization with target market specialization.

Personally, I have been in B2B my entire life, beginning in the traditional ad agency business but quickly morphing to the consulting/copywriting practice I've had for 30 years, where I've consistently charged higher fees than just about everybody else. There is, in fact, an entire directory called *Who's Charging What?* in which copywriters foolishly publish their fees—and mine (not listed there) are 4X to 100X higher. Hasn't slowed me in the least. I have also, at different times, owned a manufacturing company competing head to head with others, and been part-owner of an awards/trophy company selling to corporations, fraternal organizations, and government agencies, including the U.S. Navy, Air Force, and Marines. Never have I had these companies claim lowest prices or sell based on price, and it has generally been known that our prices were higher than competitors. In some cases, such as my consulting/copywriting practice, having very high fees is not only widely known, it's promoted as a reason to retain me if you can—if you want the best guy on the planet.

The reality of B2B commerce is that only about 20% of all purchases made by professional purchasing agents, other

executives or managers, authorized department heads, and business owners are based on lowest competitive price, and over half of that 20% occurs within the context of pre-framed competitive bidding. The other 80% of the purchases are made based on more complex criteria. That criteria ranges from the quasi-fraudulent, such as bonuses, gifts, and bribes, to simple quality of relationship to rational reasons, such as the vendor's positioning, reputation, value proposition, and added value, service, warranties, to emotional issues such as CYA for the person making the purchase or bragging rights by having the vendor. In some B2B instances "Made in the USA" once played a big role and is returning as a factor. It's new-age equivalent is "green."

Years back, a friend of mine, Pete Lillo, smartly located his print shop immediately adjacent to the area's busy post office, in a shopping center surrounded by fast food restaurants. He knew that office employees and secretaries out for noontime errands, to the post office, and to grab lunch, would drop off printing and copying work to him because of his very convenient location— without ever considering comparing his prices with other shops a few miles away, east, west, north, and south. Consequently, he quickly built and maintained a thriving, exceptionally profitable business generating approximately 300% more revenue than the national average for a shop its size, in large part thanks to prices 20% to 40% higher than other area shops. Top quality helped, but a convenient location was much more of a deciding factor in a lot of his business rather than either quality or price. For the record, accounts obtained this way, for this reason, included some very large corporations spending thousands and even tens of thousands of dollars every month on business printing.

The bottom line is: 20/80. Only 20% of the purchasing is based on competitive pricing, 80% is not. But 80% of all sellers and salespeople behave as if it was the other way around, and

devote 80% of their efforts to competing on price. This is the equivalent of having a genetic pre-disposition for a horrible disease, being shown irrefutable, empirical evidence that 80% of the reasons people with your genetic pre-disposition for the disease get it have to do with eating red meat, then making 80% of your entire food intake red meat.

As comedian Ron White says: "You can't fix stupid." But ignorance is repairable, so if, until now, you just haven't known the facts and have been pricing, marketing, and selling in the false reality of competitive pricing, that's good—you can fix yourself. And fix the way you approach your market.

Why then, you might ask, does it *seem* **so many B2B sales and purchases are made based on competitive pricing? Two reasons.** One, because that's what you believe to be true, so you see, hear, and accept everything that verifies your belief and reject without actually seeing or hearing everything that contradicts it. Two, because 80% of the marketers and salespeople in the B2B world advertise, market, and message price despite it being a purchase determinate only 20% of the time. So the noise is much about price. And the excuse ignorant or ineffective or ignorant and ineffective manufacturers, wholesalers, vendors, professionals, and salespeople give for their failures is losing a competitive pricing battle they could not win. People love placing fault elsewhere rather than embracing personal responsibility— think overweight folks and their bad genes, big bones, low metabolism, food industry conspiracy theories.

The more important question is: Why does *any* **B2B purchase get tied to competitive pricing and the lowest price?** After all, buying by price alone is rather stupid. It ignores countless other factors that may be as important. Would you choose a babysitter for your kids by lowest price, despite the fact that he's a convicted child molester or she's a drug addict? Then why choose a computer system for your company that way?

Three key factors are responsible. One is: opportunity. The easier it is for a customer to price-shop, the more tempted he is to do so. In the consumer marketplace, a person can now stand in his local furniture store with his iPhone and check the price there against Amazon, Costco, etc. instantly, online. Sears idiotically advertises that they'll do it for you, thus boxing themselves into selling at lowest price. The B2B buyer has the internet sitting on his desk, knows how to use it, and because he can, feels he should. Price shopping goods or services has never been easier, so the temptation has never been greater, nor has the pressure from above in big companies. **Two is: the surrender in advance I'm discussing throughout this chapter, which directly links to number three: Absence of other persuasive information provided by competent marketers and sales professionals**. Few buyers really want the cheapest price; all intelligent buyers want or can be made to prefer the best value. These things are rarely the same, but in the absence of persuasive information about matters other than price, shown two apparently identical items, we'll all take the cheaper priced of the two.

As example, you want a simple navy-blue blazer. If you see two that look and feel alike, and have no brand bias, and one is $199.00 and the other $499.00, surely you're tempted to shrug and take the cheaper one—even if your Bentley is being guarded outside by your chauffer. But if somebody who is articulate explains the difference between single-stitch and double-stitch tailoring, sewn versus glued, full versus half lining, why one fabric will soon look shiny from dry cleaning while the other will not, odds are very good that the jacket selling for four times more is leaving that store with you.

Now let's assume you are me and you wander into a very good clothing store with top sales professionals—like I did in Las Vegas, at the Bernini store the first time I was sold a very expensive Bernini suit. There, before you even get to the product features/benefits differentiation story, you'll be engaged in different dialogue. And you may never get to the features/ benefits differentiation, as it is somewhat assumed based on the Bernini brand, and may be rendered unnecessary by the other dialogue. That dialogue began with what I did for a living and under what circumstances I might be wearing a suit? . . . . Answer: professional speaking, on stage. What was my objective or what might come of such speaking? Answer: attracting a major client. And what might a client be worth? Answer: $100,000.00 and up. Hmmm. Having the best possible appearance, presenting a rich and successful appearance was therefore an important investment for me, wasn't it? As this conversation took place, I was de-jacketed, put in the suit coat, paraded in front of the mirror, oohed and aahed over, led to dressing room, swapped pants, measured and pinned, and had yet to even hear the price. In reality, what did it matter?

The B2B buyer is no different. In the absence of persuasive information about differential value, he will buy the cheapest product that meets his need, and he may very well go searching for it. As he should. The problem here is not the buyer. He's doing his job given what he has to work with—an absence of persuasive information other than price. It's the seller who's failing at his job—providing persuasive information other than price. It's you, not your customer.

Here is a million dollar fact for you. If you will hammer it into your head, it will easily be worth a million dollars during your career, probably more. **There is *no* B2B buyer of *any*thing for whom some factors other than price aren't relevant and important.** Please stop, think, read it again. And again.

There is the argument, of course, that the customer is simply, purely, irredeemably a cheapskate. Really? Let's take a very thorough tour of his office as well as his home, investigate which hospital and doctor handled his by-pass operation, see what car he drives, and where he stayed on vacation, etc. At his office we damn well better find the desk is nothing more than old doors secured from the city dump up on sawhorses, the bookshelves just boards on bricks, no framed pictures on walls, no brand-name copier or other equipment—all off-brand, everything bought second-hand. He better be driving a 10-year-old Yugo. His last family vacation at Motel-6 and Travel-Lodge way, way off the beach. Not the case? Then stop with the cheapskate talk. A horse is a horse, of course, of course, unless he's Mr. Ed, but no human is a cheapskate about everything. Few are cheapskates about anything when they are provided persuasive value differential information.

If you're losing price wars, you're in the wrong war to begin with.

There are but two possible outcomes to price wars—neither one victory. The B2B price competitor either bleeds and starves to bankruptcy, slowly and painfully over time, as his profit is taken away bit by bit by bit, or he loses more skirmishes than he wins, and more importantly fails at getting good customers, obtaining only bad ones.

Many companies who let themselves get sucked into this become debt burdened, financing their present poor profitability with future obligations. The young founders of a promising software company I once advised chose this path. They were charging significant up-front fees in order to have their excellent system installed and users trained, and acquiring good, committed clients by doing so. In a paean to the gods of volume and speed, they tossed aside this model, dropped their monthly maintenance fees, and took on new accounts with no up-front financial commitment. Two calendar quarters later they expressed shock that their turn-over and churn of accounts had skyrocketed, and the achievement of profitability was now stretched out many more months into the future for each month's new accounts—requiring taking on more debt. They may yet get rich, but only if a white knight arrives to buy their company. They are gambling all on that single possibility. I suppose this is a gamble made often in the software and tech fields, and the news reports the winners, but ignores the far greater number of losers. Only you can decide for yourself, as an entrepreneur, if this is the wager you wish to make with your business. But if it isn't, then the decision to compete on price or to succumb to downward price pressure from competitors is a poor one.

CHAPTER 10

Breaking Free of the Price-Product Link

Dan Kennedy

I n their minds, most business owners and salespeople tightly link price and product. The consumer, however, is very willing to break this link, given sufficient motivation.

If product and price were tightly linked in consumers' minds, Starbucks, a Rolls-Royce or Bentley, a $25 T-shirt, or Advil® would never sell instead of its cheaper, generic exact equivalent. If Starbucks was about coffee, a Rolls about transportation, a team-logo T-shirt about clothing, or Advil® about pain relief, they could not exist. Instead, all these things are, in part, about a brand identity that adds to price but adds little or nothing to intrinsic value. Further, each is about something else, and in most cases, about different things to different buyers.

Howard Schultz conceived Starbucks as a third place between home to work and work to home—the cool kids' club. A statement is made to self and others by making a Starbucks run—or having one made for you—versus bringing a thermos of coffee with you from home (the much, much cheaper substitute) or being seen with cup from Denny's, Dunkin' Donuts, 7-11, or a no-name corner store. The meaning of driving the Rolls is rather obvious, but clearly you could drive in luxury for less. A $5 T-shirt becomes a $25 T-shirt by adding some logo for which the wearer has emotional affinity or the wearer is using to make a statement. The person who buys Advil® instead of the cheaper generic that is an absolute equivalent, revealed by comparing the ingredient disclosures on both labels, often does so without comparison despite how easy, quick, and available the comparison is— because they are buying belief in safety, reassurance of efficacy,

---

NO B.S. Price Strategy Warning #4

There are two chains that bind product to price: one is in the customer's mind, the other is in yours. BOTH must be cut. It's a near certainty that the chain in your mind is bigger, thicker, stronger than the one in the customer's mind. Customers embrace de-linking product and price routinely given reason to do so. Business owners and salespeople are, ironically, more committed to the linkage. In this case, as in most, income improvement will follow self-improvement!

---

the comfort of familiarity. Interestingly, there is clinical research that reveals a "panacea plus factor" to results experienced by consumers/patients given brand name vs. generic prescription and OTC drugs, and when told the prices, from higher-priced vs. lower-priced drugs. I imagine you could have most people taste test two cups of coffee, one in a Starbucks cup, one in a 7-11 cup, and have most insist the Starbucks tastes better, richer, etc.—but have both filled with the same Maxwell House instant coffee you heated up in the microwave. A fantastic demonstration of this is the episode of Penn & Teller's outstanding exposé show, *BULLSHIT*, on Showtime, about "designer water" taste tests.

Point is, *your* product-price price-product link is in *your* mind. It is not necessarily fixed in the same way in consumers' minds. It probably isn't. Yours is more rigid, theirs more elastic and flexible. Further, the marketplace consistently displays its welcome of creative de-linking of price from product. Income limitations businesspeople live with based on prices they believe they can charge are more of their own lack of creativity and imagination, than of the products they deliver. So, as soon as you truly disconnect price and product in your own mind, the easier you'll find it to make a lot more money; the more successful you'll be in selling up, to the affluent; the less competition will matter.

This is easier said here than done. You have been firmly conditioned ever since entering whatever field you are in that a profound link exists, that there is a very, very, very short chain between product and price and price and product. Yet all around you there is abundant evidence of the error of your conditioned belief. Consider something as utterly commoditized as a head of iceberg lettuce. Surely there's no price elasticity in this lump of vegetation! In the area where I live, I can buy a head of lettuce at a Giant Eagle supermarket—where I have a choice of "organic" and ordinary at two different prices, or a third choice (shredded, in a bag), for yet a different price. Just down the road, I can buy it at a small, independent, presented as fresh-from-farm grocery, for yet a different price. Five miles or so, in summer, I have choices from a roadside stand where I can buy it direct from the farmers. Close by, I can go to a Whole Foods store and find different choices at different prices. Not here, but where my daughter lives, the farm-fresh head of lettuce will be delivered to her home along with other produce, by pre-arranged, regular, weekly delivery or by e-mail or phone order anytime—at yet another, different price. I can also go out for dinner and get half a head of iceberg lettuce with blue cheese crumbles, dressing, and bacon served as a wedge-salad, and pay varying prices—all multiples by the ounce vs. buying at the grocery and making my own salad—depending on which restaurant I choose. Geez, there are a lot of different prices for lettuce.

The exact same thing is true for ice cream. I invite you to take a look at a business I'm deeply involved in developing as I'm completing this book, that delivers farm-fresh, homemade ice cream by air, in freezer chests, to consumers all over America, from the Idaho farm and dairy, at ReedsDairy.com. You have, of course, ample opportunity to get vanilla ice cream at widely varying prices close to home—the grocery, the convenience store, a Baskin & Robbins, a Dairy Queen, a Cold Stone Creamery. But you can't get *this* ice cream anywhere but ReedAndKennedyIceCream.com.

The conditioned belief in price-product/product-price link is utterly discredited B.S., yet most businesspeople cling to it and are dominated and controlled by it as if their deepest religious belief. That thinking is very much in your way.

The Three Best Chain-Cutters

The product-price chain is best cut clean by . . .

1. Who is buying the product.

2. Who is selling the product.

3. The context in which the product is being sold.

Good news: you can control all three, to your advantage, if you will.

1: The "Who Is Buying" Matters a Lot

I've addressed one variance-of-who in great depth and detail in my book *No B.S. Marketing to the Affluent*. Different people buy the same product or service at different prices because of who they are, rather than what the product is. My example above, about being seen at the office with a thermos of coffee or a cup from Starbucks, is as good an example as any. The up-and-coming, ambitious mid-level executive at many kinds of companies dare not be seen with a thermos or a 7-11 cup. Because I sell "success" and must be a demonstration of my "product," I never arrive at a hotel where I'll be speaking to a group via an airport shuttle or cab, even if there's a free shuttle direct from the private air terminal I fly into, or it's a five-minute ride; I dare not be seen in anything but luxury sedan or limo with driver. I know a lot of people who swear they've never set foot in a Walmart store—including, famously at the time, Senator and then-presidential-candidate John Kerry's wife. Why? Because for them it's inappropriate to be there. For some, unimaginable. Even though Walmart likely carries the very same Kleenex® and light bulbs bought for their homes elsewhere at double Walmart's prices.

I sell professional services B2B. My clients range from small business owners to CEOs of billion-dollar companies. They are all very much aware there are many Walmart-like options to me, at dramatically lower fees, not to mention easier to work with, yet they hire me and I have no shortage of repeat clients and eager, patiently waiting new ones. This has less to do with what I do than who they are, and how they perceive themselves and

their businesses.

Timing + Who also matters. Parents spend considerably more money on their first baby and child than on #2 and #3, so price is automatically separated furthest from product if you are selling to them while she is pregnant with and they are raising #1 than if you're there for #3. The star athlete is much more unfettered in his spending right after signing his giant new contract and pocketing a fat signing bonus than after ten years in the league, negotiating what his agent has cautioned him will be his last deal. A person diagnosed with a disease who has a "self-help" mindset will spend more on books, CDs, online information, multiple expert opinions, and alternative health products in the first six months immediately following diagnosis than in the ensuing six years. A corporation's spending fluctuates over time in response to many factors, both internal and external; crisis or opportunity. When in a spending mood, the corporation may de-link product from price in order to get immediate rather than delayed delivery, a higher level of expertise from the vendor, or a need to make some sort of visible demonstration. The price BP was willing to spend for top Google® search engine placement leapt up dramatically immediately after the oil spill vs. before. The product: search engine optimization and placement did not change one iota, but the price BP was willing to pay for it changed overnight.

Profiting from changes in your chosen Who's can occur at any time, as often as your own open mind, ingenuity, and willingness to change permits. Profiting from changes in Timing + Who requires more alertness, agility, and at times, a willingness to be predatory.

2: The "Who Is Selling" May Matter as Much or More Than the "Who Is Buying"

With many things, what I call "leadership position" is very powerful. People prefer the trendy, talked-about restaurant because it is trendy and talked about—to the extent that their prices and others' prices are made irrelevant. In financial services, for most investors, normal levels of anxiety have been exacerbated in most recent years by the wipe-out of wealth in the markets and by government-chicanery (as with Bear Stearns, AIG, GM, etc.), bank failures, and the recession; so "who can I trust?" now has far more caché than "how much can I make?" for many. Thus reputation, evidence of stability, actual cash reserves, and leadership position have been made more valuable as assets in competition than they were several years before. A friend of mine who is one of the top New York Life agents in the entire country, Sidney Halpern, has regaled me with the anecdotal stories and financial facts demonstrating a massive stampede of money from other companies, from maturing bank CDs, from hither and yon to annuities at New York Life precisely because it is New York Life. Price/yield often is not even asked about; comparison shopping is a non-issue.

To be fair about this, leadership position does not matter nearly as much to people in their 20s and 30s as it does those in their 50s and 60s, or when extreme greed is used as the main basis for the sale, or when an entire product category is new. It is not a universally powerful factor. When it isn't, some other "Who Is Selling" factor often takes precedence.

The subject of making yourself THE "go-to guy" (or go-to company) in whatever field you're in is far too complex to tackle here. It is not the focus of this book. It is part and parcel of much of my other work, which you can sample via the invitation on page 234. Here, suffice to identify it as one of the top three factors in cutting the chain linking price to product and product to price.

If you combine #1 and #2, you can separate price from product by otherwise unimaginable distance. Just a few paragraphs before, I said this about my business:

*I sell professional services B2B. My clients range from small business owners to CEOs of billion-dollar companies. They are all very much aware there are many Walmart-like options to me, at dramatically lower fees, not to mention easier to work with, yet they hire me and I have no shortage of repeat clients and eager, patiently waiting new ones. This **has less to do with what I do than who they are**, and how they perceive themselves and their businesses.*

But that only told half the story. The other half is that who I am, and who they believe I am, greatly impacts price. They seek me out to craft advertising and marketing strategies and write copy for their advertising and agree to de-link my fees from any normal and customary modes of pricing or definitions of work product (such as hourly, by page, by item on a menu, i.e., 4-page letter costs $x, full-page ad costs $y) because of who I am. I am, for example, known as a specialist in certain things; in fact, as *the* specialist in certain things. I have, for example, longstanding working relationships with prominent, respected caché clients. I am a celebrated, prolific author on the same subjects in which I work. I have an established, on-going, somewhat paternal relationship with about 25,000 business owners and leaders who read my monthly newsletters as well as my books, attend conferences where I am featured speaker and, there, a celebrity typically signing autographs and taking pictures for hours. It is from this "base" that 70% or so of my private clients ascend. I could go on. All these things factor in to me being my clients "who of choice" to such degree that I am de-linked from price.

Before you excuse yourself as unable to create such positioning, I remind you that I am entirely self-taught and un-credentialed, entirely self-positioned and promoted, in a highly competitive field, and went from start to very high fees and high demand in under ten years. While I am very hopeful

I'll never be called upon to prove it, I could replicate that journey now in under three years. So could you. In any field.

3: The Context in Which What You Are Selling Is Being Sold Matters

The difference in price between a face cream sold at Walgreen's and a face cream sold in the home by a Mary Kay or BeautiControl consultant or a face cream sold at a cosmetic counter in Saks or Nieman's or a face cream sold in an exclusive boutique in Beverly Hills or Paris is very disproportionate to the difference in the product's ingredients. The price is governed by the expectations of the consumer largely based on where they are buying it, perhaps brand, and the expertise of the salesperson. Not the product.

I have done a lot of work as a marketing strategist and copywriter in the skin care and cosmetics industry for more than 25 years; I have even controlled a brand and had private label cosmetics and "non-surgical face lift" products manufactured for a company I owned a big stake in. The truth of this industry is that there are only a few ingredients for which claims regarding reduction in the appearance of aging, collagen production, and healing can be legally made, so every company uses the exact same ingredients. The differences are slight, in ratio, strength, and different added ingredients that bring "story value" but have negligible if any real affect on efficacy. Further, a number of different, very differently priced brands are made in the same factory with exactly the same formulas—the only difference being the context in which they are sold, and price.

Consider selling in the home, face to face, vs. selling at retail or online. For a number of years, smoke detectors were sold alone—for about $99.00 to $199.00 each—or within the context of complete fire protection systems also incorporating heat detectors, at $3,000.00 to $5,000.00 per home. Moved to the shelf at Home Depot or Walmart, the very same smoke detector is $9.00 to $19.00. Water filtration systems have experienced the same death of price. Encyclopedias were once bound books sold in homes for $800.00 or so; go online and see what it currently requires to buy into unlimited use of Encyclopedia Britannica. Or use Wikipedia for free.

If we move any of the lower-priced automobiles—say Kia or Hyundai—out of their own dealerships with dedicated sales forces into Costco and Sam's Clubs, with a buy-it-yourself system, what happens to price? It will drop considerably. But, if we take a guy adept at demonstrating a magical cooking or cleaning appliance out of a booth in the tents at county fairs and set him up in a Costco or Sam's Club, we can raise the price and sell just as many units per number of people viewing the demo.

Some years back, when I was doing a lot of work with the chiropractic profession, it was the norm for the doctor to deliver his "report of findings" or case presentation to new patients in his tiny, messy little work office or even a corner of a treatment room. I took a doctor averaging $2,000.00 for treatment programs to averaging $5,000.00 overnight with no suppression of closing percentage (buyers per presentation) and no change whatsoever in patients or his presentation but for two "little" game-changers: one, we created a "closing room"—a well-appointed, very professional looking office that stayed neat and was comfortably furnished, with a built-in light box to show x-rays and a screen to show video; two, we took him out of his casual shirts and put him in a blue shirt, conservative tie, and white doctor's jacket. A 250% price increase with no change to the product.

One other thing about the context in which the selling takes place: Sales Choreography®. This is a term coined by Sydney Barrows, my co-author of the book *Uncensored Sales Strategies*, which I cannot urge you enough to get and read, thinking about it the whole time as price-product chain cutter. In brief, this refers to the physicality of the sale. As a simple example, again in professional practices, we've documented differences in acceptance of treatment programs, price resistance, and referrals produced by no variable other than patients being called out to and summoned from the reception room to doorway to the back versus a staff person coming out into the reception room, to the person, inviting them back, and walking with them to the door.

CONTEXT means: the circumstances that form the setting for an event, statement, or idea, in terms of which it can be fully understood and assessed. Within that definition, everything matters. The cleanliness of the hands and fingernails of the staff person at the front office counter matter. And in aggregate, everything forms the basis for the customer's assessment, at conscious and subconscious levels, and that affects price. In her way-back-when, former-life business as the infamous Mayflower Madam, in its time the classiest, highest-priced escort service in New York, Sydney learned that having phones answered by a mature

RESOURCE

Sydney Barrows' book *Uncensored Sales Strategies* is available at all booksellers. Sydney also occasionally offers complementary tele-classes and other resources without cost or obligation, related to SalesChoreography® and creating extraordinary customer experiences at www. SydneyBarrows.com.

woman with a British accent made higher prices acceptable than if the phone answered by a young New York girl with *that* New York accent and, at times, chewing gum in her mouth. You might think of this as contextual congruency—everything, i.e., every little thing, fitting together to reinforce an idea supportive of a certain price.

CHAPTER 11

The Power of Pre-Determination

Dan Kennedy

I bought Dean Martin's Rolls-Royce Corniche II convertible. See page 102.

It was made for Dean. He had her from 1986 to 1991, briefly and barely driven by one person after that, then to a car museum, where she rested until I acquired her in 2010. When I got her, she had just 19,000 miles. She runs like a new auto from the showroom. Just as gorgeous. I didn't go looking for her, but when I found her by accident, that was that. I have always had a strong affinity to Dean.

Had I been looking for any pre-owned, mint condition 1986 Rolls convertible, I imagine I could have acquired one at a lower price. If I would have been happy with any age Rolls convertible or any 80s luxury convertible, certainly I could have acquired one

at a much lower price. In this case, price didn't matter and could not be negotiated. There was but one, and I was pre-determined to buy her. Some price would have deterred me, I suppose, but not the one I paid nor would have one five thousand or ten thousand dollars higher.

If I decide I want to buy a home in Florida, as I am contemplating, I can find a wide, wide, wide range of prices. If I'm not terribly persnickety about coast or inland, on the beach or just close, architectural style, big lot, small lot, in the current market as I write this, I could find a number of bona-fide bargains. There are very fine high-end, luxury Florida homes to be had at 20 to 30 cents on the dollar of their owners' purchase prices, let alone their peak values. But if I pre-determine that I wish to live in the community of Celebration, Florida, originally designed by Disney, then none of anything I just said will affect me or the price I'll pay. Everything going on outside the perimeter of Celebration is irrelevant. If enough people are pre-determined to buy within Celebration, a greater number per available property than the number per property outside its borders, then the fundament of supply vs. demand will push prices in Celebration up higher than for comparable properties outside its borders, and support those prices despite downward pressures, slumping values, and recession all throughout Florida. If I pre-determine I want to live in Celebration within walking distance of Town Square, my choices will be much more limited, which, for the most part, will push up the price of a four-bedroom box there significantly above the price I might pay for the very same box at the opposite end of the community. Sounds like the old saying in real estate: the most important thing is location, location, location. And it is, but it is also more than that; it is pre-determination about a location, brand identity, the unique small-town-Americana ambiance baked in to Celebration, and an affinity for Disney. And if I decide I'd rather live in one of the few, rare luxury homes being built by Disney, on Disney property immediately adjacent to the parks, for the first time ever, I will pay the full retail price, from $1.8-million to $10-million with no quibbling despite a depressed Florida real estate market surrounding that little community.

Donald Trump's brilliant chief negotiator George Ross observed: there's never any problem selling the penthouse. There's only one. But it's typically been even easier to quickly sell the penthouses in buildings bearing the Trump name. Some buyers are pre-determined to live in the penthouse in a Trump property because it is a Trump property.

Is this product better because it is in Celebration, or bears Disney or Trump identity? Maybe a little, but not proportionate to its higher price.

If consumers do not care, for them price matters a lot, and if there are enough consumers who do not care, price is

suppressed. Consider this book. Its value to anyone in business who makes even a little use of it is considerably in excess of its price. But it cannot be sold for anything close to its value, because of the context in which it is sold (refer back to Chapter 10), and because many buyers will not have a strong pre-determination to buy this specific book—instead they'll be shopping for an interesting book on marketing or sales or maybe even price. There are others surrounding this one on the bookstore shelf or at the online bookseller's site. If there are a number of people who will be pre-determined to buy this specific book—as there are because I have a following and I promote a new book's release direct to that following—its price can be inched up a little bit above the average or typical price of others in its category, space, and place. If I did not care about having the book published by a full-fledged publisher or about distribution in bookstores and with online booksellers—which I care about as a means of gaining exposure to virgins who are unfamiliar with me—I could print the same book myself, send a letter about it to all my followers, sell it directly to them for 300% to 500% more than the price on its cover that you paid, and keep all the money, rather than getting a small percentage of the price as a royalty. If selling only to my followers pre-determined to get my next book, I could put a much higher price on this product and everybody would still be happy. So, I pay a price for the book acting as advertising, reaching out to virgins. My followers get a bargain, as they buy the book for about a third or maybe even a fifth of what they would pay if I published it privately only for them. You paid about a dollar or two dollars more than you might have paid, had I not had the floor support of my existent followers who could be depended on to stampede to booksellers and buy a sufficient number of books to make the publisher and the booksellers happy, so that the purchases by virgins was extra.

One more example, then the all-important moral of the story.

If a florist near the entrance to a fairly large, upscale community prices a dozen roses at, say, $95.00, and has nothing but those roses available, he probably won't sell all or even many of his roses this Friday. Men stopping on impulse on the way home will judge his price way too high. They will not care enough about their impulse to pay such a price. But if somehow magic occurred and this Friday was Valentine's Day and every man had suffered from amnesia about this life-or-death holiday until the very moment he saw the florist's sign, and these men had much to lose by divorce, the florist would be out of roses in no time, outrageously high price be damned. Now, don't mess this up. The important variable here isn't the Valentine's Day holiday or the amnesia or the risk of costly divorce. They are just factors that create the state of mind that makes a high price irrelevant: caring a lot more about getting "x" than its price.

That is the state of mind you want your customers to be in when you are selling to them. This goal is everything. How you get to it may not, in your business, involve a holiday, amnesia, risk of divorce, a celebrity, or any specific item named here. It may very well involve some of the types of things named here. But the important thing is that you understand and dedicate yourself to the goal. It is the ultimate price strategy.

CHAPTER 12

The Secret to
Price Elasticity

Dean Killingbeck

I grew up in Michigan, where my family owned a 218-acre produce farm, growing corn, beans, cauliflower, and cabbage. When I turned 16, my father delegated the marketing to me—which actually meant going to market, not the kind of marketing I do now. After the two-hour drive, I had to set up, display, and price ten different products, and compete with other farmers selling the same produce, sometimes at lower prices. I quickly learned that some buyers cared only about price and that I shouldn't waste time talking with them, but that there were other buyers looking for quality more than lowest price. Over time, I found that about a dozen key buyers were taking most of my produce, at prices higher than my competitors. Armed with that information, I began circumventing the competitive marketplace altogether. I found out where they gathered for breakfast every morning, I got up even earlier for my drive from farm to city, and showed up at their favorite diner. I had most of my sales done before I or they ever got to the market.

Today, my farming is on a much smaller scale—for personal consumption. But Dan calls lead generation and customer development "farming," and I carried those earliest lessons forward to my work today, running the leading company in the done-for-them marketing programs field, helping all sorts of businesses "farm" effectively. We avoid price wars. We preserve our clients' price strategy and profits. We focus on bringing the right customers through each of our clients' doors. At age 16, I learned that all customers are not created equal. Why not zero in on the best? And circumvent the competitive marketplace altogether?

Price Elasticity means you *can* s-t-r-e-t-c-h your prices beyond those of direct competitors, if you get the right customers, the right way.

Who Is Your Best Customer?

Most business owners honestly don't know who their best customer is. They haven't done careful analysis, probably because they think they can't really control whom they attract, and they're eager for any and every customer they can get. If it has a pulse and a wallet, c'mon in! But if we know who a business's best customer is, we can, in fact, use specific demographics to select the people in its area who match up well with the profile, and then invest money in marketing only to those best customers. This makes it possible to stay out of the competitive marketplace, standing right alongside other merchants, and yelling similar, broad, often cheapest-price-based messages at all passers-by. It lets us do, on a more sophisticated level, what I did with my dozen power buyers. Go *directly* to them.

If you build your business by going after anybody and everybody, it's almost impossible to avoid doing so based on price. 80% of the people you attract this way can only be kept coming back the same way. Coupon clippers, internet junkies shopping around for discounts, and others most motivated by "deals" have to be sold that way all the time. If you are going to entice somebody to try your business out for the first time with a special offer, you need to be sure you're bringing somebody to you who matches your best customers, and can be nurtured and developed into another "best customer," with balanced interests other than cheapest price.

Here's how it works. A couple clients and friends of mine, Keith McCrone and Gerry Frank, both own auto repair shops in the Cleveland, Ohio, area. I should point out that Cleveland's economy has not exactly boomed in recent years. Three years ago, both owners decided to increase their businesses with targeted rather than mud-against-the-wall advertising. Their businesses were thriving, when competitors' weren't, because of the type and quality of the customers they had, so they reasoned they needed to get more of *those* customers—not just any customers. This is a very important principle: price elasticity has more to do with the customer than the product or the service. The price elasticity of my family farm's vegetables did have something to do with superior quality, but a lot more to do with finding the dozen buyers who cared a lot more about that quality than about price.

Keith and Gerry carefully analyzed all the information they had and could collect about their best customers—types of cars owned, age, marital status, approximate incomes, areas they clustered in and lived in, and more. They determined their very best existing customers had household incomes above $60,000.00, lived within a three-mile radius of the shops, and were married with children. A good list broker can use that kind of demographic information to find mailing lists that match. You can search for brokers and list information online at SRDS.com. You may find a local list broker via your Yellow Pages. Or, to be self-serving, you might, instead, bring your demographic profile to me and let me take care of the list-finding and the direct-mail campaigns for you. (Yes, that was a crass commercial plug.) You can also have your list analysis done for you. If you don't have a good customer list and good information about your customers, you're operating without a very important and valuable asset. Dan Kennedy says anybody who ever buys a business that doesn't have this asset is a dolt, so anybody operating their business without one is a dolt, too. He said it. If you're offended, complain to him.

Keith and Gerry found me by doing diligent research into direct-mail marketing, in search of proven campaigns. Together, we married the good, solid information they'd developed about who they wanted as customers with proven campaigns and very strong, introductory offers. Remember, promoting very strong, very appealing initial offers including generous discounts, gifts, or even free products or services is possible without destroying your prices and ability to charge premium prices going forward only if the new customers given such offers are very carefully chosen. They were also able to invest in sending out my top-quality mailings because the waste was removed from the prospect list beforehand. So, two warnings: don't settle for just throwing offers out to everybody, and don't get bamboozled into sending out cheap, cheap-looking mailers because you're dumping them on everybody and anybody.

By continuing on-going marketing to their existing customers and adding these carefully constructed new customer-getting campaigns, Keith took his shop from about $700,000.00 a year to over $2-million a year, and Gerry took his from about $500,000.00 to $1.5-million. They both tripled their sales, and are not working three times as hard for their money. In fact, they've actually increased prices five times in the space of the few years of this growth, while in the middle of the recession. Neither of them even touches a car anymore themselves except for fun, because they have the demand and profit needed to employ top-notch technicians. Their shops are able to sell their services and satisfy and keep customers even though their prices are significantly higher than competitive chains and other independently owned shops within stones-throw distance. Why? In part, because of superior service, but in large part because of the customers they bring in the doors.

In my mind, you can't separate price strategy from customer acquisition strategy. If you are bringing in customers of any and every type, interest, and motivation, this has to affect your price strategy, and will almost certainly drag you into dependence on the kind of price decisions, offers, and discounts that force your prices and profits down. If you bring the right customers in the right way, this, too, will affect your price strategy, in positive ways.

Dean Killingbeck is a popular speaker, available to talk to groups of business owners about smarter, more sophisticated marketing. He is the owner of New Customers Now!, located in Howell, Michigan, providing turnkey direct-mail campaigns for many different kinds of businesses. He is also a specialist in birthday-offers and birthday-card mailings, to existing customers and as outreach to new customers. **For a copy of his Free Report, "How To Get Good New Customers, Even in Tough Times, When Competitors Can't,"** visit www. NewCustomersNowMarketing.com/priceelasticity.

CHAPTER 13

The Making of
Propositions

Dan Kennedy

A customer's reaction to price is colored by the proposition attached to the price.

Let's be crude for a few minutes. This is reportedly Frank Sinatra's favorite Las Vegas joke: a middle-aged farmer and his wife from a rural area, who've rarely traveled beyond their hometown, save up for years and go to Las Vegas. When checking in, the farmer spots an extraordinarily attractive, extraordinarily well-endowed young woman in a slinky cocktail dress and impossibly high heels loitering near the elevators; he tells his wife he thinks he has spotted one of those working girls and is curious about the price. He goes over and asks her. She takes in his bib overalls, denim shirt, work shoes, and knows better, but tells him that it is $1,000.00 for an hour or $10,000.00

all night. He laughs and says "A THOUSAND dollars? Good lord and gee whiz, missy, when I was in the Navy and went on shore leave we never paid more than $50.00." He and his wife head upstairs, he telling her of this amazing situation. Morning comes, and the farmer and his wife come downstairs for the buffet breakfast—he attired as he was the night before, she in flowered, well-worn housedress, hair in curlers, no make-up. When the elevator stops on the way down, the same lady of the evening enters, gives them the once-over and says to the farmer: "See what you get for fifty bucks?"

So, let's assume you are single and unencumbered, not morally opposed to prostitution, willing to pay for a sexual adventure, with sufficient discretionary income and cash in your pocket to indulge just about any whim. You're at your hotel bar, one late evening when you are approached by an attractive but not, to your taste, stunning young woman, who quietly asks if you'd enjoy some company in the privacy of your room. When you inquire about price, she responds flatly: $300.00 an hour. While you're mulling it over and she visits the powder-room, let's replace her with a better salesperson, who happens also, to your taste, to be stunning. When you inquire about price, she quietly says: "For the most incredible, mind-blowing, unforgettable sexual experience of your entire life—including sex secrets passed down through generations back to the ancient Orient—$1,000.00." Which price might seem better to you? Clearly one is cheaper than the other. One is 300% higher than the other. Price may make or break this sale if you are one of those rare birds who only buys by cheapest price. But it's more likely, if the sale is made, it will be by the woman who presented the superior proposition.

And so it is in the overwhelming majority of situations. Of course, I'm not suggesting that you are the equal of a lady of the evening plying your trade at the bar, although, with Sydney

Biddle Barrows, once the infamous "Mayflower Madam," I did co-author a sales book, *Uncensored Sales Strategies*, which I suggest as an eye-opening read. But don't take offense. Take the very valuable lesson. In the above situation, price matters little. If we moved the example out onto a street corner, with street hooker and guy in a car, price might very well govern the sale. Thus, **place and buyer have an impact on both price and its impact on buying decision, so you want to present yourself in a good place to good buyers. Then, price's importance is dwarfed by proposition**. And here's the biggie: you probably can't actually control all your competition, restrict all your costs, and muster sufficient efficiencies in order to always, profitably offer the cheapest price. But you are in total control of the strength of your proposition.

Five Kinds of Propositions

There are five kinds of propositions to concern yourself with:

1. *Unique Selling Proposition (USP)*. Your Unique Selling Proposition can be found in the answer to my copyright-protected

5 Propositions

1. Unique Selling Proposition (USP)

2. Unique Value Proposition (UVP)

3. Irresistible Offer

4. Unique Safety Proposition (USP)

5. Unique Experience Proposition (UEP)

question: *why should I, your prospect, choose to do business with you vs. any and every other option available?* You need a continuing USP for your business and, often, additional USPs for different products, services, offers. In a sense, this is a concise summary of your positioning. It's best if it telegraphs benefits. You can review a detailed presentation about USP in my book, *The Ultimate Marketing Plan.*

Implicit in your USP, from a price strategy standpoint, should be the answer to a second question: *why should I, your prospect, choose you regardless of price, be unconcerned about price, and never consider comparison shopping based on price?*

If you have solid answers to both those questions baked in to your primary sales message, you have the foundation for aggressive pricing.

2. *Unique Value Proposition (UVP).* This includes presentation of price, and justification/minimization of price by various means, including, when bundling, the higher value of components if purchased separately; the value of the benefits to the user; money to be made or saved through ownership of the product or use of the service. The best value propositions find ways to make price a non-issue or to make the product pay for itself. An example of the latter is the new, energy-efficient windows that pay for themselves through lower electricity bills. The task is to make a *believable* case for value far in excess of price.

Remember that value encompasses intangibles as well as tangibles. If you hire a private VIP guide to escort you around at Disney World in Orlando, you still ride the same rides, see the same shows, eat in the same restaurants, buy souvenirs in the same shops as you would without the guide. There aren't two different parks. The core tangible remains the same. But the $195.00 an hour

VIP guide delivers different value to different customers. There's status, showing off, and bragging rights; there's speed and convenience, so it's less tiring and stressful, thus making the whole excursion more enjoyable; there's being able to do more in the time you're there, thus making the whole vacation more valuable. And so on. Don't leave out all the intangibles when you build your value proposition—or when you price.

3. *Irresistible Offer*. Never forget: you *aren't* doing direct-response advertising or direct marketing unless you extend a specific offer. But a bland, vanilla, ordinary offer isn't much better than no offer at all. You have to ask yourself what *your* customers will find irresistible. For example, we know from split tests that, when selling conferences to doctors, free airfare and lodging is much more persuasive than a discount of equal value. You have to know your own customers' psyche. A complete I.O. will often include discount, premiums/bonuses (plural), incentive for fast response, penalty for response after a deadline.

4. *Unique Safety Proposition (USP)*. This usually revolves around a guarantee or guarantees, warranties, providing risk reversal or risk reversal-plus (e.g., *double* your money back), and can be supported statistically—years in business, numbers served—and with social or peer proof—testimonials, client lists. The greater the skepticism, the stakes, and/or the present resistance to spending, the stronger and more reassuring the Safety Proposition needs to be. Sometimes, this can be the basis of its own profit center. I recently bought a modestly priced piece of jewelry from a catalog. The catalog copy included a 60-day "She'll Love It Or Your Money Back" guarantee. When ordering on the phone, I was also given a one-year replacement warranty—if the item got damaged, the chain

broke, the jewel dislodged, the surface scarred—they would replace it free. I was upsold a two-year extension of the replacement warranty for "just $49.00 a year." I'm confident selling these $98.00 pieces of paper is more profitable than selling the $395.00 pieces of jewelry.

A lot of people are subconsciously if not consciously looking for safety, security, and certainty in an unsafe, insecure, and uncertain world. The recent years' chaos in all major institutions—government, banking, rock-of-Gibraltar companies like General Motors, the Catholic Church, etc., and in the economy, has left a lot of people feeling very anxious. Just about everybody has also had plenty of experiences where service after the sale is hard to come by, promises made before the sale forgotten. Into this environment you come with your proposition. Making it feel very, very safe to buy can be very compelling, and can support premium pricing.

I rack up some fat Fed-Ex bills, since I send most of my work for clients and a lot of correspondence that way. I could save tens of thousands of dollars every year by using UPS, USPS Priority Mail, and other alternate carriers. Why don't I? Because the security of knowing FedEx will get it there on time is worth more to me than the difference in cost between them and lower priced competitors. Every time I fill out a FedEx airbill, I'm buying a Safety Proposition.

5. *Unique Experience Proposition (UEP).* This is the newest proposition on this list, acknowledging the reality of The New Economy as an Experience Economy, where people most willingly buy and pay premiums for complete, total, enjoyable, and unusual experiences. People want to be assured of a good experience when buying *and* from the deliverable. Pay attention to the Experience Proposition

put forth in TV commercials for Norwegian and Carnival Cruise Lines, dining at Outback Steakhouse, or marketing I've assisted with at KennedysBarberClubs.com. None of these are restricted to or even put primary emphasis on the core products or services: the cruise, the steak, the shave 'n haircut.

In the seminar and conference business, where I do a lot of work as a consultant, a copywriter, and occasionally as a speaker, excellent, high-value educational content has gone from the thing being sold to the minimum ante to even be in the game. To motivate attendance, a complete experience has to be offered—which may include book signings with authors, meet 'n greets and photo opportunities with celebrities, field trips to interesting sites, contests and competitions, award ceremonies, car and vacation giveaways, and more. At recent years' Glazer-Kennedy Insider's Circle™ annual Marketing and Moneymaking SuperConferences, we've featured celebrity speakers including Gene Simmons of KISS, Ivanka Trump, and Joan Rivers; actors in super-hero costumes roaming the exhibit area, taking posed photos with attendees; chair-massage therapists on duty; and a VIP Lounge for a certain level of Members. A special seminar I did in conjunction with my *No B.S. Wealth Attraction in The New Economy* featured a pirate theme—pirate décor, pirate ship backdrop for photos, pirate hats and toys for attendees, plus an opportunity to be photographed with Dean Martin's Rolls-Royce (which I own), and a Night at the Races.

Ultimately, you will build a hybrid proposition, incorporating some or all of these five. For clarity's sake, you'll want to lead with the one you think serves you and fits your target market best, with the others hooked to it.

Maybe the most important thing about this for anyone inexperienced with *direct* marketing is that **you begin thinking**

in terms of making propositions. Most business owners do not. Most merely advertise the existence of their business or products or services. Or its existence plus features/benefits. Or existence plus products/prices, like car dealers' or electronics stores' advertisements do. These types of marketing messages are so common they encourage commoditization and either focus on price, suggest price shopping, or fail altogether. There are very few people who care that your business exists—beyond your spouse, ex-spouse getting alimony, creditors, and possibly somebody who awakes that day with an emergent need for what you do and is in hot pursuit of it. Likewise, for the features and benefits of your products. It takes more than that to stir up interest. The making of a good proposition goes a long way.

Even in hard core, down 'n dirty direct response advertising— the sale of a product in a two-minute TV commercial ending with "call now"—there has to be a composite of factors properly assembled for success. If you didn't see or don't remember the lessons from the TV show Pitchmen that ran on the Discovery Channel, featuring behind-the-scenes making of the famous Billy Mays commercials, I suggest obtaining and watching the DVDs. In the first episode, you are there when the inventor of a new shoe insole arrives, a commercial is planned, script written, commercial filmed and tested. You will see Billy and his partner figure out dramatic demonstrations for the insole's shock absorption: Billy pounding his hand, protected by the insole, with a hammer; a car being driven over his hand, protected by the insole. The price is decided on, in part based on an impromptu focus group of car mechanics trying out the product and being asked what they'd pay for it, as well as competitive pricing in retail, and Billy May's experience with products on TV. The proposition is then built, to stack value far in excess of the price. All that is then combined into a powerful, persuasive two-minute commercial that grabs attention, interests you in gel insoles even if you had zero interest in them before the commercial began, delivers a USP, suggests a UEP, and presents a UVP. A home run it is. Hundreds of thousands of pairs of the insoles have been sold since, with that commercial.

Depending on what business you *think* you are in—tax preparation or taxidermy, dentistry or detailing of autos, industrial chemicals or investments—you will quickly conclude the gel insoles example has nothing to do with you. If you had a conversion here and realized you are *actually* in the business of making compelling propositions, then you would find the gel insoles example fascinating. And if you took that conversion seriously, and committed to learning all you can about making propositions, and brought that to your business, you would find that selling at higher prices and profit margins becomes infinitely easier.

RESOURCE

If direct marketing is new to you, get the rules of the road and examples in every category of business in my book *NO B.S. DIRECT Marketing for NON-Direct Marketing Businesses*. To continue a thorough learning experience with me, get the *No B.S. Marketing Letter*. Membership information, page 234. If creating Unique Experience Propositions and selling more creatively interests you, get the book *Uncensored Sales Strategies* that I co-authored with Sydney Barrows, available at all booksellers, plus complementary tele-classes on creating exceptional experiences at www.SydneyBarrows.com.

Avoiding
Apples-Apples Comparisons

Dan Kennedy

Two roadside vendors are situated right next to each other, both selling fresh-picked apples from their orchards. Each has good parking under shade trees. Each has good, visible signs. Each has several people there working so service is fast. Who will win the day? Sadly, probably, the one who lowers his price below wherever the other stops.

If you choose to conduct business in this kind of situation, frankly, there's little Jason or I can do to help you. Neither of us carries psychiatrist credentials.

One year, I ordered a Valentine's gift for my wife from a catalog sent to me by Calyx Flowers. Even though, at the time, I owned stock in 1-800-Flowers and have, several times, been a speaker on the same programs with 1-800-Flowers' CEO, Jim McCann, I purchased a $199.95 gift from their competitor. My reasons are very instructive. First, they sent me a catalog in the mail, while 1-800-Flowers relied on e-mail. I do not use e-mail and I wasn't planning to send flowers as that year's gift, so I would not have pro-actively gone back to 1-800-Flowers to shop. The unsolicited catalog had a chance because it arrived and snagged my attention. As Woody Allen famously said, a third of all success is showing up. Of course, e-mail is a lot cheaper to send than full-color printed catalogs (my thoughts about the handicap of bad economics are in Chapter 16).

Unique Value Proposition in Action

The gift I bought from Calyx was a "bundle" of three gifts in matching red silk boxes, delivered one per day, over three days, February 12, 13, and 14. Absent this creative offer, I might have bought one gift, and spent less. They sold three. Many might have balked at the bundle of three for $199.95 if delivered as one, but the delivery of the three gifts over three days, building up to the finale on the 14th was unique—thus a distraction from price and an added value. Ultimately, they took themselves out of clump of flowers to clump of flowers, apples to apples comparison territory altogether by changing one little element: delivery. The "bundling" of multiple items is a common way to try and boost transaction size and make direct comparison difficult, and it alone should always be considered. But Calyx went a clever step further.

Their marketing and price strategies wizards deserve applause. Unfortunately, their implementation folks got demerits. The person taking my order over the phone was ill-informed and inept, making me wish within minutes that I'd stuck with good old, reliable 1-800-Flowers. He actually said: "Gee, they just threw me on the phones and I'm not really sure of what I'm doing." It took a l-o-n-g 20 minutes to get this order done and, yes, I should have bailed out but by then, dammit, I wanted *this* thing. Also, no attempt at an upsell. No query about a second gift for daughter, sister, mother, mistress. Sad thing is, the $199.95 thing could just as easily be $229.00, and the extra money invested in better phone scripts, personnel, training, coaching, and supervision.

(Again, see Chapter 16.) My advice: Don't strive to sell your stuff as cheaply as you can; strive to sell it as effectively as you can, and price to support whatever is required to do that.

By the way, I've never ordered from Calyx again—despite receiving countless catalogs. I have returned to 1-800-Flowers.

Nevertheless, Calyx's marketing and price strategy is brilliant. It perfectly illustrates the power of One Little Thing Changed, in getting you out of the apples to apples comparison territory. This must be your goal: escape apples to apples. Searching for your One Little Thing is a very big thing.

> ## "Little hinges swing big doors."
>
> W. Clement Stone, self-made billionaire via a direct-sales insurance company launched in the Great Depression; founder, *Success Unlimited* magazine; colleague of Napoleon Hill (*Think and Grow Rich*), author, *The Success System That Never Fails*.

CHAPTER 14

The Place Strategy That Easily and Automatically Supports Premium Prices

Dan Kennedy

A merica divides into niches and subcultures. Every individual belongs to at least one of each, but most belong to several of each. Understanding how that niche or subculture membership and affinity stretches the price elasticity of just about all goods and services can put a great deal of otherwise lost money into your bank account. With bravado but no reluctance, I'll promise that this chapter alone can be worth millions of dollars to you over the remainder of your time in business, and could provide a dramatic, fast income improvement.

Simplistically, niches are occupational and vocational; subcultures are by interest, belief, activity. So, insurance salespeople a niche, deer hunters a subculture. Most divide into sub-niches and sub-subcultures, as do these. There are life insurance salespeople, property and casualty insurance salespeople, specialized property and casualty—such as those serving only farmers or only construction companies, or those insuring collector cars and rare art works. There are deer hunters who use only bow and arrow, who hunt only in the Midwest. Most people have very strong identification with and affinity to whatever niches, sub-niches, subcultures, and sub-subcultures they belong to. They tend to buy a lot of things somehow linked to those niches and subcultures. In fact, it rarely takes a Sherlock Holmes to wander around someone's office or home and, by the objects on display, detect what niches and subcultures the person is part of. In my large home office and library, for example, you will find a plethora of Disney books, collectibles, and memorabilia; advertising books, collectibles, antiques; harness racing photographs, paintings, objects; more than 50 clocks, many unusual; a small collection of rare or first edition books all in the success philosophy genre. In my garages, three classic cars. This provides hints of four subcultures and one niche to which I belong or self-identify. And to all that you say: so what?

Here's the obvious yet often overlooked fact about all this, that directly affects price strategy: I will pay more for a product, object, or service specifically, precisely "for" any of those four subcultures or my professional niche, than for a generic equal of the same product or service, and I will rarely if ever question whether a cheaper generic will do just as well. To put it another way, the movement of a product or service from generic to niche or subculture automatically permits price increase, with no change in the actual manufacture or delivery cost of the product or service. You might want to stop and read that again.

We'll do a business product first, from my arena of publishing. Let's assume I have a product consisting of six audio CDs recorded at a seminar, with an accompanying manual and workbook, *Effective Time Management*. What is its price? If you go to the online catalogs of companies that publish such products, such as Nightingale-Conant Corporation, you will find that a low of $39.00 to a high of $79.00 is the prevailing price range. The same information, condensed and commoditized as a book can be found at a bookstore for about $9.00 to $15.00. But, if my product is *Effective Time Management for In-Field, Territory Sales Professionals* and it is advertised in some media they read, then it may easily carry a price of $179.00 to $379.00. The number of CDs didn't change, nor the size of the manual, so it cost the same to manufacture, yet it will sell for 300% more, give or take. If it becomes *Effective Time Management for In-Field, Territory Salespeople in the Gardening Center and Hardware Store Industry*, its price may again double. Its price is based not so much on what it is, and definitely not on what it costs to make, but on who it is for, the fact that it is for someone specific, and that they believe they and their needs are unique and automatically respond better to what is just for them vs. what is for anybody and everybody. Key word: *automatically*.

Now to consumers. In the same magazine for dog lovers (a subculture), I saw a big ad for nice ladies' gold pins, earrings, and bracelet charms, of cute little doggies selling for $19.00 to $39.00, and a different ad from a "collectors' gallery" of the same type of jewelry, but available in images of 20 different breeds, so you get the jewelry that precisely matches the pooch you own. That jewelry priced from $99.00 to $199.00. If they had included "Schnoodle" as one of the breeds, I would have ordered jewelry for my wife, as that is the breed of our designer dog, affectionately known as The Million Dollar Dog. They didn't, so I didn't. I did not order the lower-priced generic dog-image jewelry either. The $39.00 and $199.00 pieces are comparable in size, overall appearance, 24 KT gold-plated, and warranty, but one sells for 500% more than the other.

This is our famous Million Dollar Dog. She has her own leopard-skin couch, an upstairs and a downstairs bed, and flies by private jet, but refuses to eat gourmet or organic dog treats, preferring doggie junk-food snacks you can buy at Walmart. Go figure. Just as trivia, $45.5 billion was spent on pets in 2009, up 5.4% from 2008, despite recession. $3-million of that went to Doggles.com, a maker of high-fashion sunglasses for dogs to wear at the beach.

In the professional practice arena, my long-time friend and "student," Dr. Gregg Nielsen, advertises his Back-to-Work Treatment Program, his Auto Accident Injury Recovery Program, his Anti-Stress Treatment Program, and other specifically named treatment programs. All involve essentially the same chiropractic treatment. But if you've been injured at work, which strikes you as more valuable: ordinary chiropractic treatment available anywhere or the Back-to-Work Treatment Program? If he were to take that a step further and market an Almagam Industries Back-to-Work Treatment Program to employees of Almagam Industries via the union, free lunch-and-learn presentations at the factory, and direct-mail to the employees at home, he would virtually negate all competition and make price, certainly competitive price, irrelevant.

The deeper the commitment to niche or subculture, the less price matters for the precisely matched product, so the more price elasticity exists when moving a generic product to the niche or subculture. I own, train, and drive Standardbred horses in harness races. I have also owned Thoroughbred racehorses. These horses are different breeds, but both are racehorses, with more similarities than differences. Their owners and trainers, however, inhabit two entirely separate subcultures and, generally, do not like or respect each other. The exact same liniment or potion for the racehorse's sore muscles or nutritional supplement to boost the horse's stamina will have virtually the same impact on either breed of horse, engaged in either type of racing. But if you are the manufacturer or marketer of the liniment or the supplement and you are so tone deaf and dumb as to name and package it the same for both markets, put a generic horse's head or both types of horse on its label, and run the same generic ad in both the Thoroughbred and Standardbred trade journals, you'll be selling those products for half what you could be selling them for, maybe even less. You could command a significantly higher price from each subculture community by presenting yourself and your product as exclusive to each of them. Were I advising such a client, two separate companies would be formed—say Thoroughbred Stamina Laboratories and Standardbred Stamina Laboratories; two different product packages made with two different product names—say Kentucky Derby Performance Power (for the Thoroughbreds) and Hambletonian Performance Power (for the Standardbreds), and two different ad campaigns made, with only testimonials from Thoroughbred trainers in one, only testimonials from Standardbred trainers in the other. And never the twain would meet.

Too much thought about price is tied to tangible factors, as Jason describes in Chapter 7. Too little thought given to

COIN OF THE REALM

Owner: Kennedy Sports Corp.
Driver: Dan Kennedy   Trainer: Clair Umholtz
Condition Pace - Purse $1,600   May 29, 2010
28   57.3   1:27.3   1:58.2

JJ ZAMAIKO PHOTOGRAPHY © 2010

Yes, this is me, driving professionally in harness races at Northfield Park (NorthfieldPark.com), as I do about 200 times a year. PRICE IS NEVER AN ISSUE when acquiring a desirable horse, buying veterinary or chiropractic care, the best nutritional supplements, or best equipment. That's how everybody feels about something, and one of the finest price strategies of all is connecting what you sell with buyers who feel about it, or can be made to feel about it, that same way.

intangibles, notably including the customer's perceptions and feelings about the product. Even with theoretically pragmatic, practical B2B buyers, feelings play a profound role in most buying decisions, and most reactions to price. In the liniment and nutrition example just above, there's no difference in the two products bottled for the two different subcultures. The only difference lies in the buyers' feelings about the product. Because it is presented as formulated specifically and exclusively for the buyer's type of horse, he has more confidence in its efficacy and therefore in its value than he would in a generic product, so he is naturally agreeable to paying a higher price for it.

Isn't There Something "Wrong" with This?

So we arrive at the ethics question. Someone reading this is disturbed, thinking I'm advocating charlatanism or outright fraud, or over-charging without commensurate benefit. Neither is true, but even before getting to that, I want to remind you of your chief responsibility as owner of or salesperson for a business: to maximize its profits, within the boundaries of the law. If you are emotionally uncomfortable with that, you should not be running a business or acting as its representative; you have a conflict of interest. If you have trouble with that, I urge getting and reading my book, *No B.S. Wealth Attraction in The New Economy.*

Now, to the matter of fraud. Nothing I did here comes close. The product named, packaged, and advertised as formulated to improve the stamina of the harness racing horse is, in fact, formulated for that purpose and has that effect. The fact that the same formula does the same thing for a different type of horse— so what? It is of no concern to the harness horse trainer and should be of no concern to me as its manufacturer. It is not only an irrelevant fact but a distraction that might actually deter that trainer from getting a helpful product. The most ethical thing I can do is present this beneficial product in the way most likely to be accepted by this customer. The least ethical thing I can do is let him wander off never trying my extremely beneficial product or buying inferior products because I'm a lazy, timid, or inept marketer. As to the idea of over-charging without commensurate benefit to the buyer: nonsense as well. The benefit to the buyer is two-fold: first, getting him to buy the beneficial product in the first place, and, second, creating sufficient confidence and enthusiasm in the product that it doesn't wind up idle on a shelf, but is used, used as instructed, and given a long enough trial to demonstrate its benefits. That *is* value. That is worth money. Even if there was a dollop of charlatanism in the selling, if there was true benefit derived from the use that would never be experienced without the charlatanism, then the charlatanism itself has value and is worth money.

NO B.S. Price Strategy Warning #4

There are two chains that bind product to price: one is in the customer's mind, the other is in yours. BOTH must be cut. It's a near certainty that the chain in your mind is bigger, thicker, stronger than the one in the customer's mind. Customers embrace de-linking product and price routinely given reason to do so. Business owners and salespeople are, ironically, more committed to the linkage. In this case, as in most, income improvement will follow self-improvement!

De-linking value in your own mind from the ingredients in the bottle and whatever **they cost, and from the fact that some product comprised of those exact same ingredients may be readily available at a substantially lower price, is essential**. Thinking inside that box severely constrains your price strategy, and misses the truth about value; that it is about the result(s) experienced by the buyer, or, in some cases, the experience itself, or even just the feelings experienced by the buyer. This value is naturally and automatically, and often substantially, increased for the buyer of a product he experiences as "expressly for" him and his niche or subculture vs. a generic, and that entitles you (*if* you need permission) and empowers you to attach a substantially higher price to it. You are pricing to value.

I call this a place/price strategy, even though it usually does not relate to geography as place (although it can). By place here, I mean the niche or subculture, and the existent state of mind of the customer within that niche or subculture. In every respect, place has a great deal to do with price. In geographic terms, the same service may carry a much higher price in Manhattan than in Boise, the exact same product a higher price at the mall in La Jolla than at the mall in Indianapolis. In fact, I can find the same sweater in the same store in a mall in Akron, Ohio, and in Beachwood, Ohio—about 30 minutes' drive between them—at two different prices, because one is a more affluent community than the other. A stand set up for a bake sale to benefit a local cause may find need to sell at lower prices if set up on the sidewalk in front of a Walmart than if set up on the sidewalk in front of a Target. But there is something called "media geography," too. The person with a low-mileage, mint-condition 1960 Chevy will most likely sell it for a higher price if he advertises it at web sites and in magazines for Chevy aficionados and collectors, than if he advertises it in his local Pennysaver, the bulletin board at Denny's, or even on eBay. Often, the place strategy that can have the greatest upward influence on price is the move from generic or mainstream to niche or subculture.

Business Soars, Selling to a Subculture

I'm always fascinated to find an entrepreneur who has found a "place" in which to conduct business where price doesn't matter and a product/service/proposition for which price is virtually irrelevant. The company called MOTO-ART (www.motoart.com) is there. Their specialty is furniture made from actual airline parts—the DC-9 wing desk @ $9,600.00, glass top $1,400.00 additional; the TBM Avenger conference table made from the WWII war plane's rudder @ $12,500.00; a curved desk made from the engine cowling from a #727 @ $6,800.00; or a love seat for two made from that same cowling, same price; my favorite: an executive desk chair from a B-52, complete with ejection seat apparatus—*"don't like what you're hearing in the office, just pull the lever and abort"!*—$4,900.00. That's a chair for five thousand bucks. Gotta be some profit in that! The company's sales are driven by its own cable-TV show "Wingnuts," and the ease with which they can secure free publicity in countless magazines—although targeted direct-mail is easy for them to do, as lists of licensed pilots, airplane owners, private air terminal operators, and subscribers to pilot and plane owner magazines are all readily available.

The Lessons Are These

1. It's about the "who"—when the right person sees their catalog, there's something in it he MUST have. *Must.*

2. It's product made for a very specific Who.

3. It's not just a thing, it's a cocktail party story, an opportunity to show off; it's about a person's passion to which he is profoundly committed. Therefore . . .

4. Price does not matter. The prices of ordinary coffee tables, conference tables, chairs are completely irrelevant; this is in a category-of-one.

5. They have more than one target market to live on: they are B2B, with private air terminals, charter company offices, and companies in the airplane manufacturing and travel businesses as potential clients—reached directly and via commercial architects and interior designers; they are to-consumer, with active and retired private and commercial pilots, aircraft owners, and aviation aficionados as customers.

Their position is enviable. The trick is NOT to reject that position as out of your reach, but to scheme to navigate your business into that very same territory.

If you reverse those five factors supporting their high prices out of a business, you arrive where price is always an issue in the mind of the buyer, likely challenged and suppressed by competition and commoditization.

CHAPTER 15

How "The Company You Keep" Can Impact Price

Dan Kennedy

The most interesting thing about price is the wide range, from very low/cheap to very, very high/ expensive there is for just about every product and service. For every price there seems to be buyers. One of the most important truths about that variance in price for the same product is that it is greatly affected by things other than the product.

One of these factors—available to just about every marketer— is **The Principle of Association.**

You are probably well aware that TV and movies are, today, much about what is called "product placement." If Shrek drinks a particular brand of soft drink or James Bond drives a particular automobile in the movies, interest in that product soars and sales increases usually follow. It's not foolproof, but it's real, and hundreds of millions of dollars are now spent on it. When a celebrity is seen wearing certain apparel, even a shade of lipstick, or using a product, again, sales often benefit. Sales of both shoes and sunglasses that Sarah Palin was seen sporting during the 2008 Presidential campaign got a huge boost. This associative effect on sales is well known. What you may not have been as aware of is that association can affect price as well.

A great example of a company that knows this and uses it to advantage is Allen Brothers, a purveyor of very expensive, prime steaks and other foods, delivered to your door. They sell predominately by mail order, with their own catalogs and website. Steaks are, I remind you, a commodity. There is at least one supermarket within a short drive from your house where you can get steaks for your cookout, minutes before firing up the grill if you decide on impulse. There is probably more than one such store near you, and there may be an independent, old-fashioned butcher shop in your area as well. There's also a big dog in direct marketing, Omaha Steaks, which, like Allen Brothers, sells steaks by mail. Their prices are higher than the supermarket, but about half what Allen Brothers charges. You can also get bargains on steaks at Costco and Sam's Club. Home shopping TV fans know you can buy steaks on QVC. There are even Donald Trump-brand steaks sold on QVC and in several catalogs. Steaks at very low, low, moderate, high, and Allen Brothers prices. Maybe there's someplace you can spend more for steaks than Allen Brothers, but I've not yet found it and it has not yet found me.

My wife is rather frugal, so we buy a lot of steaks and other meats from Omaha Steaks, for our day to day dining, and order from Allen Brothers more for special occasions, especially if having friends over for dinner. Common, odd behavior, if you stop to think about it—treating guests better than you treat yourself. It should be the other way around.

Anyway, how does Allen Brothers make their higher price appropriate? One way is with the Principle of Association. Their catalogs usually feature a list of famous, top-tier steakhouses from all across the country, that buy their steaks from Allen Brothers. One of their catalogs I kept in my advertising files prominently displayed the logo of a different top steakhouse on every page. This reinforces their basic promise: by buying from them, you can have the same exceptional quality steaks that the very finest (and most expensive) restaurants serve their customers—at home. This suggests that, at their prices, you are actually getting a bargain, if you compare to the prices of dining out in these restaurants. (See page 122, Avoiding Apples to Apples Comparisons). It also has them selling bragging rights and the cocktail party story, something affluent customers respond to. When your guests praise the steaks, you can say "Well, we have them flown in overnight from Allen Brothers. Have you heard of them? They provide the steaks to Mortons."

Look at everything Allen Brothers accomplishes with their association to the top steakhouses:

- **Differentiation**, from all other purveyors of steaks
- Makes their extremely high prices a **bargain by comparison**
- **Makes it "OK" to spend so much**—you're saving by dining in
- Frees them to price as they wish—without concern over competitors' prices
- Gives their customers **"pride of ownership"** of something judged by experts (the top steakhouses' chefs) to be the best
- Gives their customers **a bragging-rights story** to tell

Obviously, the restaurants buy from a different division of the company, at very different, wholesale prices. I do not know this, but it wouldn't surprise me if Allen Brothers gave them additional discounts in order to make use of their names and logos. If need be, it would be money well spent.

Any business can do this, at national or local level. The specific association tactic used by Allen Brothers is getting and bragging about cachet clients. The great ad man David Ogilvy got great self-promotion mileage out of having Rolls-Royce as his client. For many years, a lot of business came my way—with little or no fee resistance—because it was known in direct marketing circles that the Guthy-Renker Corporation was my client and relied on me for advice, advertising copy, and script writing. (Guthy-Renker is the firm behind celebrity-filled TV infomercials and the leader in that field.) Many decided for themselves they wanted the guy who was Guthy-Renker's go-to guy. It's important to understand that association not only brought clients to me, but facilitated my charging my chosen, way-above-par fees. Similarly, my 9 year's tenure on the best-known, largest public seminar tour, drawing audiences of 10,000 to 35,000 in 25-plus cities a year, brought me a lot of other speaking engagements from corporate and association clients—and made my compensation requirements a non-issue.

At a local level, it is often easier to leverage the cachet client. If it is known that Mrs. Rich-Britches, the number-one star of the local social circuit, patronizes your boutique, all the women at her country club and in her circle will follow suit, as will women who only know of her. Diana Coutu, operator of Diana's Gourmet Pizzeria, makes much of being the official pizza provider of the local, very popular hockey team, of having diabetic-friendly pizzas endorsed by doctors and nurses of the top area hospital, and of her own competing in and winning awards in international pizza chef competitions. It is not coincidental that her prices skew quite high—as of

> # NO B.S. Price Strategy
> # Warning #5
>
> **A lot of emphasis is put on product, proposition, and price, and rightfully so, but never lose sight of how important the prospect's perception of the seller is**—of the seller's expertise, status, authority, etc. Two different merchants can present exactly the same proposition to the same prospect, and one be met with enormous resistance (and price resistance) and the other met with unquestioning acceptance.

this writing, from $22.00 to $38.00 for a large, specialty pizza. Her business doubled from 2008 to 2009, incidentally, despite that thing you might have heard was going around, recession. (See more at: www.dianasgourmetpizzeria.ca.)

At the local level, the boost from any national prominence can be extraordinary. My friend Mike Storms, who owns a thriving martial arts academy near New Orleans and gives private martial arts, mind-set, and success coaching to executives and entrepreneurs, is flown in to work with a couple NFL teams and a top college football team, and has several NFL athletes as private clients. I hope he won't mind me revealing this, but he under-charges these clients by necessity (as there are many eager to replace him who would work for free, only for the glory) because the associative effect is very beneficial to him in his main businesses back home. It is not coincidental that Mike's student fees at his academy are the highest of any competing school nearby or any within a 100 mile radius, and his private coaching fees run into the thousands. (See more at www.stormskarate.com.)

There are many ways to develop these associations, beyond the scope of this book to cover in detail. Obviously, you can make a point of pursuing influential customers or clients. Create a "top 50" list of local celebrities, owners of well-known and respected businesses, influential civic leaders, and the like, and keep them on your mailing list, invite them to every event your business hosts or sponsors, send them articles that may interest them; make yourself and your business visible to them, persistently. You may be able to volunteer your services as a resident expert to some organization, charity, or event, that provides promotable bragging rights or good networking opportunities.

By all means, be alert for opportunities. One year in one of the cities that the big seminar tour I mentioned went every year, a young limousine service owner was in the audience. Afterward, she wrote to the seminar company owner and many of the speakers, offering to provide free limousine service the next time the tour came to town. My client, who owned the company, took her up on her offer. The next year, she chauffeured many of the celebrities appearing on stage with us—they're a blur, but I believe that time, in that city, that included Mary Tyler Moore, George Foreman, Larry King, the famous defense attorney Gerry Spence, and the famous business speakers Zig Ziglar, Brian Tracy, Tom Hopkins, and me. She got her photo taken with each of us, standing by her limo, with its logo on the door visible. She used this to get some very good publicity immediately: a feature story with the photos in the local newspaper, and an interview on a top radio program. It all migrated to her website and brochure. Instantly hers became "the limousine service of the stars" in that city. On my advice, she raised her prices to a point above all competition.

Another friend of mine, Jordan McCauley, is an expert in connecting entrepreneurs and marketers with celebrities. In his outstanding book _Celebrity Leverage_, he explains exactly how even small companies can, for very modest sums, get their products in the backstage gift bags given out at Hollywood awards shows, given out in

> **RESOURCE**
>
> Visit Jordan McCauley's site, CelebrityLeverage.com, for information about putting your products in the hands of celebrities and making your business famous.

celebrity gift suites at various events, and otherwise put into the hands of celebrities. This tactic has helped unknown, small jewelry and fashion designers, cookies and cupcake bakeries, children's products inventors, and many others leapfrog to prominence. Keep in mind this all impacts on price as well as demand. Jordan tells, for example, of jewelry designer Amy Peters succeeding at getting her jewelry worn to a movie premiere by an actress in the movie _2 Fast 2 Furious_, having several Survivor contestants seen wearing her jewelry in photographs in a number of magazines, and having her jewelry worn on the TV show, _The OC_—all thanks to sending out gift baskets direct to celebrities, exactly as described in the book. When she migrates that to her website, catalog, and blog, and provides it to retailers who might carry her line, it not only spurs interest and demand, but tends to make price a non-issue.

In almost every case, fame not only fosters interest and spurs demand, but also diffuses or negates price or fee resistance. Fame _is_ a price strategy. You can get this benefit by making yourself famous or by association with other famous people, companies, organizations, or brand-names.

CHAPTER 16

The Deadly Trap of
Bad Economics

Dan Kennedy

To a great degree, I run a M*A*S*H* unit for wounded marketers. Just like on the old *M*A*S*H* television show, periodically sirens go off, and my assistant, Vicky, yells "Incoming!" Because I am so expensive, a lot of clients foolishly wait until they are in trouble to come to me. At that point, what they usually want is to quickly get from me a better, more powerful and effective ad or direct-mail campaign or integrated offline-online campaign to counteract their collapsing sales and dwindling profits. That is rarely what they need, though, because—make a big, bold note somewhere—great marketing cannot overcome bad economics.

One way a marketer arrives at these dire and desperate circumstances is bare-bones pricing and buying customers

with aggressive discounting. When you handicap yourself with bare-bones margin, you have no money for effective, aggressive advertising, marketing, and promotion to acquire customers, for "wow-factors" customer love, or for retention after the sale. So handicapped, the business owner's response to every meaningful suggestion that might provide competitive advantage, differentiation, and power in the marketplace is met with: "We can't afford that." Hire a celebrity spokesperson? We can't afford that. Advertise on the top syndicated radio programs that are real market-makers? We can't afford that. Pay me to craft extremely effective sales copy? We can't afford that. Put superior salespeople in the stores, do more on-going training and coaching, retain a good mystery-shopping firm? We can't afford that either.

Yes, you can drive sales with bare-bones pricing. But you cannot sustain success that way.

Oh yeah, Kennedy, what about Walmart? First of all, Walmart's rise to power was based on multiple factors including a superior, more efficient distribution system. It is perpetuating lowest prices in certain categories now by virtue of giant-sized status, allowing the squeezing of every ounce of blood out of suppliers, forcing overseas manufacture, and even getting manufacturers to place their brand names on inferior products made to Walmart specs. Historically, though, the bigger they are, the harder they fall. There have been Walmart-like bullies before, now extinct and forgotten. But regardless of the future sustainability of Walmart, should you use them as your model, you better be able to do *everything* they do. You can't just decide to mimic them as lowest-prices-every-day leader in your field without also having extraordinary efficiencies in your business, the power of epic size, and the ability and willingness to force your vendors to sell to you at bare-bones prices. Be careful when you copycat that you *can* copycat. (Elsewhere in this book, my co-author, Jason has more to say about Walmart and how small retailers successfully stand up to the bully, and even prosper in its shadow. I also urge reading a dated but still relevant book, *Up Against the Walmarts* by Don Taylor and Jeanne Smalling Archer.)

If you saddle your business with bad economics, please don't direct the ambulance you're in to my M*A*S*H unit unless you're ready for a price strategies fix, not just an advertising operation!

Just what are "bad economics"? Pricing, thus profit margin and profit in dollars ill-matched with the way you need or want to advertise, market, promote, and sell, the clientele you want to attract, the customer experience you need or want to deliver, and your own financial objectives. Simply put, there has to be enough money to do what needs to be done.

The owner of the Italian restaurant in the city, who makes the decisions to hire the very best chef he can attract at a very stiff salary, fly in fresh fish daily, import cheeses from Italy, keep the house small so the dining experience is intimate and over-staff to provide flawless service is going to have to make a lot more money per plate of spaghetti than Olive Garden does. If he tries matching their prices or is even influenced by them, he'll lack the money necessary to do what he has set out to do. Conversely, if you're going head to head with Olive Garden and

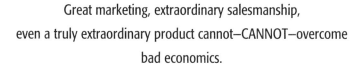

NO B.S. Price Strategy
Warning #6

Great marketing, extraordinary salesmanship,
even a truly extraordinary product cannot—CANNOT—overcome
bad economics.

targeting middle-income, middle-class families, you can't layer on a top chef, made-from-scratch meals, imported cheeses. You'll be broke in a New York minute. All that seems as obvious as a meatball, yet countless business owners in every imaginable field err in creating economics ill-matched with their approach to their business.

If, for example, you are going to sell a product via direct mail or television infomercials, certain economic realities exist. Cost of media inside cost of sale is going to be very high—perhaps 70% to 90%. You need a 300% to 500% mark-up from cost of goods. If it costs $3.00, it must sell for $9.00 to $15.00. But if your thingy costs $20.00 to make and there's no way anybody can be persuaded to pay more than $59.00 for it, you can't use direct-mail or TV. Your economics will not let you. Period. End of story. If, however, you are only going to market the product by placement in others' catalogs and at others' websites or via online affiliate programs, a thinner margin may be just fine. Different media, different economics. Generally speaking, the tighter the margins, the fewer the marketing options, the slower the growth of the business, and the more vulnerable it may be to somebody bigger 'n badder taking notice, and swooping in with a competitive product with better margin, which allows him to spend more and do more to make a sale.

This book is loaded with ways to transform bad economics to good economics. In the above example of products sold on TV, you might alter those economics with immediate telephone upsells, padding shipping and handling or, if well-capitalized and investment minded, being willing to incur a small loss for the customer acquisition offset by profits in subsequent sale and list rental. It's not where you start that matters but where you wind up, with price strategy. In direct marketing, I rarely panic after test marketing to determine the cost of selling whatever is being sold, even if it is appreciably higher than can be tolerated.

Between the cost to make the sale and what can be spent to make that sale may be a crevice or a canyon. Either way, as a marketing strategist, I then go to work on bridging the gap.

As example, drawn from a real situation, but changed just enough here to protect a company's proprietary data, let's assume we are selling a book about "100 ways to live to be 100" by direct mail to well-targeted lists. Testing proves that $49.00 is the best price; anything higher, response drops like a boulder. Anything less, response does not significantly improve. But at $49.00, it costs $70.00 to make the sale. The gap is $21.00 + cost of the book itself + desired profit. So, $21.00 + $4.00 + $5.00. Gap of $30.00. If we can bridge that gap, there are 100,000 names per calendar quarter to mail to, and about 4,000 books to be sold; $20,000.00 profit to be made—plus whatever we might do afterward with these customers. In this scenario, we can get rich, if we can bridge the gap. As a side note, the smallest local business has this same sort of challenge anytime it is going to reach out creatively and aggressively for new customers.

In this case, here's how we bridge this gap:

Five "sponsors" are found who agree to have "bonus chapters" about their products inserted in the book—each paying $1.00 per book for that stealth advertising plus the list of buyers. There's $5.00 of the $30.00.

The offer is changed: the book at $49.00 or the book plus a documentary DVD about longevity and an interview with the authors for $59.00 ($10.00 added/cost $2.00/net $8.00). 20% of the buyers chose this option. $8.00 x 20% = $1.60 of the $30.00. Now we've covered $6.60 of the gap. A third option of the book plus the DVD plus a 3-month supply of an anti-aging nutritional drink mix is added—at $99.00 ($50.00 added/cost of DVD plus drink mix $12.00/net $38.00). 10% of buyers take this option. $38.00 x 10% = $3.80 of the $30.00. Total: $5.40 of the $30.00. So now $12.00 of the $30.00 gap is accounted for.

A cosmetic company is brought in as a joint-venture partner; they add a DVD infomercial to the package at its expense, selling a $300.00 "system" of age-reducing complexion care products. They pay the book publisher $100.00 per sale. 6% of the book buyers buy the skin care products. $100.00 x 6% = another $6.00 per book buyer.

At that point, we've bridged $4.00 + $5.40 + $6.00, total $15.40 of the gap. Remaining gap: $14.60. We're roughly halfway there. Going back to the drawing board on price strategy, we test "2 payments of $29.00" vs. the price of $49.00. It does not suppress response, and causes very few non-payment or collection problems. Factoring those in, the net gain is $7.00. The gap is now down to: $8.00. By using the same "2 payments" and a slight price bump with the other offers—book+DVD, and book+DVD+drink mix, another $2.00 in net is snagged, reducing the gap to $6.00.

At this point, the publisher is feeling confident enough to find and hire a celebrity to endorse the book, who could be used in the direct-mail piece, for a cost of $25,000.00 per year divided by 16,000 units of sale, worsening the gap by $1.56. But as we both expect, it cuts $5.00 off the cost per sale, a net gain of $3.44, leaving a gap of only $2.56.

In a final act of desperation, we increase the regular shipping and handling charge by $1.20, and offer a new, expedited shipment option for another $1.60 on top of basic.

Whew.

There are now 16,000 sales to be made per year at a $5.00 front-end profit, putting $80,000.00 net profit in the bank. There are also 16,000 customers with known interests, who will buy books, DVDs, and products related to health and longevity. There is no cost of acquiring these customers again; new and additional books can be created and brought to them, repeatedly. If this entrepreneur were to average an annual net profit per customer of only $10.00 after the fact of the first sale, that first year's crop of customers would yield $160,000.00; the 2nd year, 32,000 customers yield $320,000.00; 3rd year 48,000 customers yields $480,000.00. With reasonable spending restraint and prudent savings, this fellow is a cash-in-the-bank millionaire in under 5 years.

A much bigger publishing business that operates in the health arena very much along these lines (although not the basis for this example) is Rodale Books. If you are curious about all this, beyond illustration of bridging the gap, you might look them up online. And, if you're curious about the self-publishing and information marketing businesses, check out the Information Marketing Association at www.info-marketing.org.

OK, I know that was exhausting. But the willingness of the business owner to work at bridging gaps is a big factor in success or failure, especially if trying to grow and expand a business. For many businesses, bridging a gap is not so complex and arduous. But even if it is, the asset owned afterward can be well worth it.

The most important thing to exit this chapter with is an *attitude*: that bad economics may be transformed to good economics with sufficient cleverness and effort if the pay-off is worth the effort, but that you want to avoid saddling yourself with any poorer profit margins and profits in dollars than absolutely necessary—so there's enough money to be aggressive with marketing.

Welcome to Math Class

Class is in session—and you would rather be outdoors, playing. Or doing just about anything but math. I get it. I empathize. But this isn't ordinary math. This is Money Math. Essential and profitable.

How a 10% Price Increase Doubles Profit

Assume you sell a $100.00 item, with $50.00 cost of goods, another $10.00 in fulfillment costs, a $20.00 cost-per-sale for advertising and marketing, and $16.00 allocated to fixed over-head. Your profit is $4.00. If you can sell at just $10.00 more, but incur very minor cost increases—say $5.00 in cost of goods, $1.00 in fulfillment, and no increase in the cost of making the sale or overhead, your profit jumps to $8.00. The 10% price increase created a 100% profit improvement. Maybe that's not exciting to you in the $4.00 to $8.00 neighborhood, but add zeroes and look at it as $400.00 vs. $800.00, or $4,000.00 vs. $8,000.00.

How To Go Broke with Rising Sales

In their book *How To Sell at Margins Higher Than Your Competitors*, leading authority on price-preservation in B2B selling, Larry Steinmetz, and my good friend, the late Bill Brooks, assert that "most entities that go broke do so during a period of *increases* in sales volume. This statement shocks most people because everyone believes businesses fail as a result of lack of sales. However, business is not a game of volume; business is always a game of margin. If a business doesn't maintain gross margin at an adequate level, it is going to go bust—regardless of sales volume." Here's their illustrations of three ways margins can get away from you:

#1: If you cut price by $5.00 to sell something:

	Dollars	%	Dollars	%
Sales	$100	100%	−$5=$95	100%
Cost of Goods	$65	65%	$65	68%
Gross Margin	$35	35%	$30	32% (−3%)

#2: If you fail to raise price when costs go up:

	Dollars	%	Dollars	%
Sales	$100	100%	$100	100%
Cost of Goods	$65	65%	$70	70%
Gross Margin	$35	35%	$30	30% (−5%)

#3: If you find costs going up $5 and only raise your price by the amount of your cost increase:

	Dollars	%	Dollars	%
Sales	$100	100%	$105	100%
Cost of Goods	$65	65%	$70	67%
Gross Margin	$35	35%	$35	33%[*] (-2%)

[*]*Note*: your dollar gross margin stays at $35, but your gross margin as a percentage of sales goes down from 35% to 33%. In short, raising your price the same dollar amount as your cost increase is a de-facto price cut. You must raise your selling price the SAME PERCENTAGE as your cost increase percentage if you are to maintain the same gross margin percentage in face of rising costs.

At first blush, you may look at Larry and Bill's chart and think: no big deal. 2%, 3%, even 5%, in the grand scheme of things, so what? But there are two big so-what's. First, a lot of businesses operate at net profits as low as 5% to 20%. If you operate at 20 and drop 2, oops, your take-home pay just took a real 10% haircut. Second, if this turns into a pattern of mis-calculating or ignoring the true effects of margin and margin-by-percentage, it will re-occur, and a 2% drop followed by another 2% drop by another 2% drop = 6%. But if you operate at 20%, that's a take-home pay haircut of 30%.

How You Can Make as Much or More Money Serving Fewer, Better Customers

In his seminars, Larry spends a lot of time on many examples of this, because it is such a scary and difficult concept for salespeople and business owners to wrap their heads around. You CAN afford to lose a shockingly, mind-bending amount of volume and still make as much net money from minor price increases that drive away a quantity of customers. A typical example from Larry has a company "suffering" a 27% decline in gross sales, from $1-million to $729,927.00, produced by a whopping 34% drop in the number of units-of-sale/customers served, yet preserving the same net profit—from just a 10% price increase. Space here prohibits showing that entire math example or others, nor do I want to replicate Larry's excellent work. I refer you to: LawrenceSteinmetz.com. Here, take my word for the math for a moment, and consider the implications. It's possible that less infrastructure, fewer employees and the headaches that come with them, or shorter weeks or fewer hours' open for business, a lot fewer customers or clients—discarding the worst and keeping the best, less stress, and time to craft and deliver excellent products/service could yield as much or more net, take-home income. This is how Price Strategy can translate to personal benefit and lifestyle improvement, not just different numbers on a financial statement.

Clever Math = Same Excitement, Lower Cost, Better Profit

Keith and Travis Lee at American Retail Supply and 3DMailing Results.com are brilliant B2B marketers of promotional merchandise and turn-key promotion campaigns for all kinds of businesses as well everything from store shelving to routine supplies for retailers. Here's a clever discount strategy they used. "Most marketers simply do a percentage—20% Off, 50% Off. We used to do that, then switched to running occasional discount promotions with a set dollar discount at various order size points. But as you can see in our anniversary promotion (shown at end of this section), we actually DECREASED the percentage as the order size went up. Counter-intuitive yes. More profitable, also yes. The $40.00 off order up to $200.00 equals a maximum discount of 20% but the $80.00 off an order up to $500.00 provides a maximum discount of just 16%. Buy more, save $40.00 more but 4% less. Results: 47 clients placed orders averaging $2,026.26 and took advantage of the $80.00 savings—just a 3.95% discount given. (Total sales: $95,234.22). 78 other clients took the $40.00 discount, average order was $278.47, yielding an average discount of 14.37%. (Total sales: $21,720.66). Had we done a straight 20% OFF promotion, we would have given up $16,507.97 in discounts that, instead, stayed with us. You might speculate that offering 20% OFF rather than the set $40.00 and $80.00 might have produced more than enough extra sales to make up for that $16,000.00, but in our experience, based on careful testing, that is not the case. In fact, the flat 20% takes that full bite out of every added dollar of revenue without compensating benefit. We've had enough experience with this in our business to know that the flat dollar amounts off, tied to order size, create just as much response and volume as did % offers."

This is the kind of sage advice that Keith and Travis give their 3DMailingResults.com clients, and share in their local area as Glazer-Kennedy Insider's Circle™ Independent Business Consultants, with local Chapter members.

This is a perfect example of how the very same discount promotion idea can be implemented with slight variation, yet the Money Math differential is substantial. One slight tweak, $16,000.00 of additional profits captured or $16,000.00 of additional, unproductive expense incurred.

How To Run Your Numbers

The dilemma: if you raise prices, sales could fall—as with Larry's example—but will that bring less profit or more? If you cut prices, you need to know how much sales need to increase to compensate for your margins—which have probably shrunk further than you think. Microsoft Excel® can help you do the math. An article/ tutorial, *How To Use Calc-Plots To Plan Pricing Strategies*, and related tools can be found at ExcelSolutions.com, ExcelUser.com, and in an e-book, *Dashboard Reporting with Excel* by Charley Kyd. These resources enable you to create different price increase/

decrease, units of sale, and margin scenarios and have them depicted graphically for you by plugging in numbers.

Hate To Crunch Numbers?

Me too. But here's a fact from my 30+ years of doing marketing consulting with business owners: those making the most money, especially those growing businesses from small to big and getting rich by doing so, know their numbers inside and out, thoroughly, completely, and just can't be stumped by a numbers question. Those who can be easily stumped are usually poor or headed there. In addition to the above resources—studying Steinmetz, and getting and using Excel tools or something like them—I urge reading Chapter 42: What IS Profit, Anyway? And Chapter 43: Management By The (RIGHT) Numbers in my book, *No B.S. Ruthless Management of People & Profits*. Chapter 43 explains the 13 most important numbers to watch like a hawk, most of which are not well-understood by your accountant, because these are the numbers you use day to day to make money, not the numbers you use after the fact to calculate if you made money.

RETAIL MARKETING NEWS

AMERICAN RETAIL SUPPLY

Kent, WA • Denver, CO • Honolulu, HI
Call 1-800-426-5708 • Fax 1-253-859-7300
www.AmericanRetailSupply.com

Volume 17 Issue 6 — December 2009

Celebrating Our 40th Anniversary!

Savings Certificate
You Save $40.00

when you order $200 or more.
Savings double to $80.00 with your purchase of $500 or more.
Offer Expires January 7, 2009

Call 800-426-5708 to redeem your Savings Certificate
You must mention this unique offer number 97774 to receive your $40.00 savings.
You must mention this unique offer number 97775 to receive your $80.00 savings.
When you order online at www.AmericanRetailSupply.com enter 97774 or 97775 in the
Promotional Code box at check out.

Keith Lee
President, American Retail Supply

One of the first lessons I learned from Dick Thompson, the founder of American Retail Supply, when I started working here as a sales rep in 1978 was, "in business, you only get in direct proportion to what you give." That's one reason everyone here at American Retail Supply understands who the boss is.

Everyone here knows that **you** give us every pay check we'll ever get. **You** give us every pay raise. **You** pay for our vacations, and our kids clothes and **you** put every gift under our tree this Christmas... and that's why we're going to do everything we can to make sure that we Make-**You**-Happy every time. **Remember, Only Happy Clients Come Back,**
Keith Lee,
Owner, American Retail Supply.

*Do What You Do So Well
That People Can't Help Telling
Others About You*
Walt Disney

In 1970 the lunar spacecraft Apollo 13 splashes down in the Pacific after near catastrophe, Richard Nixon is president, 18 year olds are given the right to vote in federal elections, Love Story is the top grossing film, "The Long and Winding Road" becomes the Beatles' last number 1 song; and Dick Thompson starts Thompson Marking Service which will become American Retail Supply.

1

Do It All!

As you might know, I do some marketing consulting. You've probably heard the adage that the teacher learns more than the student. Frankly, that's the main reason I became a Glazer Kennedy Insider's Circle Independent Business Advisor (GKIC IBA) and marketing consultant. I wanted to be sure I kept growing and learning about marketing.

A few weeks ago I was consulting with a client in regards to his Lost Customer Campaign. A Lost Customer Campaign is a marketing campaign to get lost clients back. Since it can be a long time between purchases, this client considers a customer lost if they haven't bought from him in 18 months.

My client does a pretty good job of staying in touch with his customers but I saw an opportunity to do something really eye opening that recognized clients *(Continued P2 - Do It All)*

Front Page of the 40th-Anniversary promotion newsletter featuring the $40/$80 discount offer.

CHAPTER 17

How *Do* You Set
Your Prices?

Jason Marrs

This is what it all gets down to: Picking a formula. **Setting a price.**

As you walk through your store, page through your company's catalog, examine your own website or "mystery shop" your salespeople, you realize there are dozens if not hundreds of price decisions that have been made. Were they made according to a formula? Do they reflect a conscious, thoughtful price strategy? Do they successfully land in the sweet spot, just at or below the highest price a sufficient number of your customers will pay, but no lower? How do you know? Have they been fairly tested? As you think about the prices you now charge, can you explain—and defend—how you arrived at them?

As sad as it may seem, if you walk into most businesses in the world and ask their owners or presidents how they set their prices, they'll probably stare at you blankly, with a look in their eyes that reminds you of that deer in headlights right before the truck plows over it. If they eventually can enunciate their price-setting strategy, it will almost certainly fall into one of five very rudimentary, common categories.

One: WAG

The most rudimentary method for setting prices is called WAG, which stands for Wild-Assed Guess. Just like the name sounds, you make a guess as to what the price should be based on intuition with no formal testing, solid information, or history to guide you. You just decide you are going to sell something. You guess at what people will be able and willing to pay. You pull a price out of your butt and hope for the best. If you're lucky, you establish prices you're able to get and that don't bankrupt you. But you have no idea of how much available profit you are letting slip by. More often than not, this is a financial train wreck waiting to happen.

How Most Business Owners Price

1. WAG

2. Industry Norm

3. Clients Dictate

4. Cost Plus

5. Target Return

Two: Industry Norm

The most prevalent form of pricing is by industry norm. *Hey, what's everybody else around here doing—I guess I should do that.* Many industries even have published norms and prices or pricing formulas and it is frowned upon by peers or organized groups within the industry if you deviate from them, especially if you deviate up. This is particularly pervasive in professional businesses such as, but not limited to, healthcare (where my wife and I have our main business) and law. But it exists in many other places. That is why I'm going to spend a bit of time talking about it here.

Industry norm pricing ignores the costs and profitability of those companies being copied. It assumes they know what they are doing and that you can copy it blindly yet profitably. This, a dangerous assumption, since, give or take, only 5% of the business owners in any population prosper while 95% either struggle or fail. The number one cause of a business's slide from success to failure to extinction over time is erosion of profit margin thanks to failed price strategy—not the advent of new competition, inability to get capital, or other reasons popularly believed in or offered as excuses. To make matters worse, most often business owners using this model will take a look around and pick a price in the middle. They believe that a price in the middle is safe. It is not. A price in the middle does not have any competitive advantage. It destines you to mediocrity. You will probably have too small a profit to improve, innovate, grow, expand, or withstand trouble. You'll be better and stronger than the worst and the poorest, but inferior and weaker than the best and the strongest.

If you are following industry norms it tells me that you have no clue about what your customers really value. If you do not understand that, then it is only a matter of time before someone like me comes into your market. I will identify the value drivers of your clientele and take customers away from you so fast that it will make your head spin, usually charging them significantly higher prices to boot.

One way or another, everyone wants to be a part of something special. Customers want something they are proud of buying, of being a part of. Anything that takes you away from exceptionalism in favor of middle-of-road mediocrity and sameness has to be very seriously questioned, and that is exactly what industry norm pricing does.

Industry norms can be very intimidating. There can be illusion of law. But with the exception of actual, verified laws enforced by regulatory agencies with teeth, you should only look at industry norms as interesting information to be considered along with a variety of other information, including, most importantly, that obtained from real customers, not peers and self-appointed industry authorities. I have always made a sport out of breaking industry norms, and push my clients and coaching-program members to do the same. Our rule is: Just because other business owners have agreed to participate in a collective form of mental illness doesn't mean you must too.

Industry norm pricing can be a starting point, but it can never be permitted to box you in. Keep in mind, too, that a number of widely accepted industry norm price strategies you see today were radical, revolutionary, and reviled in their infancy. This includes all-inclusive vacations at on-land resorts, fractional ownership in real estate and other categories, fixed price and pre-paid treatment programs in chiropractic, BOGO in retail, seat license fees in sports stadiums, and many more. This means that the radical, revolutionary and, by peers, reviled price strategy you invent today may eventually become a commonly accepted norm in your industry.

Three: Client-Dictated Pricing

Client-dictated pricing is also very common. Occasionally, it's the clever basis for a good business—think auctions, where the owner is profiting from commission on gross regardless of net profit to sellers, or by providing its own fixed price services to sellers, like eBay. But in most businesses, it's just plain dumb. Driven by the myth that the customer is always right, the business owner sets out to survey customers about the price they would pay for a given item or service. From that data they set a price. This ignores the fact there is a difference between any customer and the right customer, obtained in the right place at the right time, and ignores the profound difference in reactions to price depending on the salesmanship used in presenting the product and its virtues. Surveying is basically price testing without sales presentation.

It is also against customers' own self interest to tell you the maximum price they'd be willing to pay. Let's say I have a widget, and you really want my widget so much you'd pay $100.00 for it. If I asked you, would you volunteer that? No. You want to maximize the amount of value you receive. You will tell me a low-ball price with hopes of getting it. There is a big difference between what people say they will do and what they actually do. Just because they say they will, or will not, do something does not make it true. Humans are funny that way. They'll tell you what they think you want to hear or what is in their best interest a lot faster than they'll tell you the truth. Often they won't even know the truth until they are in an actual, real situation.

You certainly do want to listen to your customers, obtain all the input and information you can from them, and give it careful consideration. Surveys, focus groups, even casual conversation with customers can be valuable. But putting people with no interest in your profits in charge of your prices is a bridge too far.

Four: Cost-Plus Pricing

C**ost-plus pricing** is a slightly more advanced way to set prices that is used by many successful companies. It is an old and accepted, albeit antiquated, model for pricing. You can find it in textbooks. If you ask your accountant for advice on setting your prices this is likely the method he'll trot out. To use cost-plus you must first determine all of your costs and then add your desired profit, to arrive at price. In its defense, this is the first rational model we have discussed. It is the first to even consider costs and profit.

While this is a significant improvement over WAG and client-dictated, there are still a lot of problems with this model. The first problem is that it assumes that consumers take into account and are affected by the costs of providing what you are selling or the profit you make—tiny or huge.

They do not care about your costs. Just because you have spent a boat-load of money on something does not mean they will have a drop of interest in buying it. What you spent developing it or spend delivering does not equate to value for the consumer. Your costs are totally meaningless to the market. If it costs you $200,000.00 to build a viable all-electric car, that won't help persuade consumers they should pay you $201,000.00, $250,000.00, $300,000.00 or even $100,000.00 for it. That's your problem, buddy. They don't care about your profits either. If you can make that car for $500.00, they'll still happily pay $25,000.00, maybe $40,000.00 for it. Whether you profit big, profit small, or lose money isn't their problem either. They care about the value they receive, period. (Value broadly yet personally defined.)

Another example: you don't take into account how far away from work the waitperson serving you lives in deciding to tip nothing, 15%, 20%, or a generous, higher amount. But if Susie lives 30 miles away and Barb lives just down the street, it costs Susie a lot more to deliver service. Why don't you investigate this and tip appropriately? Because it has nothing to do with the value you receive. You uncaring, selfish lout.

Cost-plus pricing is inherently flawed because it focuses on two things that have little or no influence on what the customer will gladly pay: cost and profit.

The even bigger problem with cost-plus pricing is that it constricts how you think about price. Cost plus forces you to focus on costs and not value. While it is designed to give you a profit, it does nothing to maximize your ability to illustrate and collect the value you provide, nor to give you the maximum possible profit. It limits you by its starting point. It pulls your attention away from the customer to the bucket of bolts bought and used to make the object being sold.

Beyond all that, it also does not really account for costs in the correct way. It totally ignores volume. As you know costs tend to fluctuate depending on volume produced or purchased from vendors. In most cases, volume lowers cost. But in some businesses, there's a curve, when delivering more volume suddenly demands big investment in equipment, inventory, staff, adds borrowing costs for capital, and actually raises costs for some period of time. Having a cost-plus method of pricing ignores that reality. It also ignores the affect price may have on volume. It's also easy to leave out opportunity costs—if we sell a lot of X, are we selling less of Y, even though Y is much more profitable to sell than X? If so, the loss from Y has to be amortized and accounted for as a cost added to X. Finally, it's easy to miss differential costs of the same product or service dispensed by different people, or by different means. For example, many businesses in the child health industry provide homebased services. Very few of their owners charge a different rate for a home visit. They will charge the same fee if they go to the client's home as they would for an office visit. They ignore the costs of driving to an appointment. They miss the fact that there are opportunity costs of being in your car and not in the office. It never occurs to them that when in the office they can see clients back to back with no down time. When going to the home they lose a minimum of 15 minutes on each side of the appointment that could have been used to see another client. Without counting wear and tear on the car and other problems that home visits create, ignoring this cost would steal a minimum of $125.00 per visit from our top line, in our business, and the bottom line cost would be even more significant.

If you are going to use or at least consider cost plus numbers, you'd better be very careful to calculate true cost.

Five: Target Return

The fifth basic pricing model is **target return**. This model looks at a business and its prices like an investment. Target Return requires you to set a target return on capital invested into a venture. So if you invest $100.00 and you aim to collect $200.00 after expenses this would be a form of target return. Simplistically, it would set price at $300.00. In reality, the time cost of money, and other factors would affect that price and might make it $310.00 or $323.62 or some other number. While it does move more focus to the profit side of the equation, it carries with it many of the same problems that cost-plus pricing has. It can also ignore the realities of the market by being too focused on a profit that may be unrealistic. Still, this is the set of numbers you want to very carefully consider, with strong emphasis on return on investment.

This last model also best allows for incorporation of your costs of making the sale as well as costs of goods and fulfillment. If you have an advertising and marketing budget of $50,000.00 a month, and you average 1,000 transactions a month, you might divide and get $50.00 invested, that must be added to the cost.

If your ad budget attracts new customers but also brings past customers back, or promotes a variety of products, assigning it in pieces to different products gets trickier.

Surprisingly, few business owners work backwards from the income they want to make per week, month, year, etc., then looking at numbers of transactions that must occur, products that must be sold, customers acquired, and *therefore* prices that must be charged to hit the income target. When forced to do so, they quickly realize their price strategy can't produce the income they want. Then the work begins.

Why Static Prices Are Impossible

Aside from not using an effective method to set their prices, most business owners tend to treat their prices like Ron Popeil's much-advertised rotisserie: they want to "set it and forget it." This is particularly true of those who use the WAG and industry norm models. If you are using those methods, let me ask you, when is the last time you checked the prices of your competition? It's been awhile hasn't it? I'd bet good money that you and most of your competition are ignoring the reality around you while your profits are withering on the vine. Inflation and your costs are completely indifferent to your lack of action. They move with or without you. That is why you can't have static prices even if you never change them. It does not matter if you keep the number the same, your price still changes. That is because inflation is affecting the purchasing power of your dollar. Every up-tic in inflation is a drop in your price. Of course that means for every up-tic in inflation your costs are moving up and your profits are going down.

Considering the spending spree Washington has been on, you can expect future inflation to be substantial. I don't care what they tell you in the news; you can't flood the market with dollars without consequence. For you, profit margins, take-home profits, and the prices that produce them are meaningless if they don't fluctuate to compensate for changes in the true value of the dollars being paid, and the costs of what you want to buy with those dollars.

Objectives of a Particular Price Point

If you now realize that businesspeople don't pay enough attention to how they set their prices, you can only imagine how little attention they pay to the *purpose* of their prices. While price is merely the dollar representation of the value you provide, its objective is always to make a profit. It could be about taking a loss today in order to make a bigger profit tomorrow, but it is always about making a profit. To take that a step further, the price point you pick aligns you with a particular strategic objective.

Those who prefer to set high prices often use a pricing method called Skimming. It got its name from milk. If you take milk straight from the cow and let it sit for a while, the cream will rise to the top. The objective of price skimming is to serve those customers at the top because they are the ones who are willing and able to pay a premium. They are the cream of the market.

For this strategy to work, price cannot be their primary concern. They must be concerned with some other form of value. It can be exclusivity, quality, or something else, but it has to exist. This applies to my healthcare business and its clients, evidenced by its prices being a substantial premium over the typical competitor. Very rarely do we get price shoppers. When we do they grab their chest and gasp for air when they hear our prices. We do our best to keep them away, and to attract only those for whom price is not a concern. Our internal philosophy is that we'd rather provide the best therapy possible than provide the most therapy possible. Everything we do is aligned with that attitude. We're in the results business. That is one of the key values we provide. Ironically we don't promote that, our clients do. Our reputation is that of being expensive but worth it.

A couple of other examples of skimming would be prestige carmakers such as Rolls-Royce and Bugatti. In case you don't know, Bugatti sells cars for over $1,000,000.00 each. Clearly their market is not even remotely concerned with price. Simon Cowell from *American Idol* has the Bugatti Veyron. He is one, only one, of the 6,000 people in the world that this carmaker estimates can afford the $1,700,000 price tag. If it strikes you as a drawback that they have only 6,000 potential customers in the entire world, don't lose sight of the advantage of only having 6,000 prospects, knowing exactly who they are, and knowing a great deal about why they buy. Don't lose sight, either, that selling to just 1% produces $102-million.

You do not need a price as high as the Bugatti to utilize skim pricing. You just need to focus on the cream of your market and not be concerned with producing large amounts of volume. Price skimming is about small volume by nature. Only certain people within the market can afford to be a part of the club. They have to be your focus if your objective is to skim the cream. My co-author, Dan Kennedy, has always run his private practice as a consultant and direct-response copywriter this way, much the same as I run our therapy practice. In Dan's case, there are lot of marketing consultants renting themselves out for a few thousand dollars a day, and traveling to their clients (thus incurring considerable opportunity cost—one day's work equals two or three days of travel); Dan charges $18,800.00 per day and makes clients come to him. There are a lot of copywriters creating ads and direct-mail campaigns for fees in the $5,000.00 to $15,000.00 range; Dan routinely commands from $50,000.00 to $100,000.00 and up, plus royalties. The pool of prospective clients for Dan is much, much, much smaller than for the other consultants and copywriters, but he knows who they are and he is rather easily able to make sure they all know of him. He has written much about this in his book *No B.S. Marketing to the Affluent*.

Sequential Skimming

Another related method is called sequential skimming. Just like skimming, this method starts with skimming cream off the top. The difference is that once demand dips because the top has been skimmed, so does the price. It drops down a level in order to stimulate more demand. It stays at that level until demand drops off and then the price will be reduced to increase demand for the next lower level of buyers. This goes on until the demand for the offering is exhausted.

The most obvious examples of sequential skimming can be found by looking at electronics. Think about plasma televisions. They came out and were priced high to attract the early adopters. The early adopters ran out and paid the price to be the first kids on the block that could hang their television on their wall. They were a little bummed out when they realized that the TVs didn't last long and were prone to have images burnt into the screen. That gave them reason to run out to buy the new and improved models when they came out. So what happened to the old models when the new ones came out? Their prices dropped to an acceptable level for the next market. This trend continues today. Flat panels have prices reminiscent of the old tube-TVs. As of this writing it seems the next generation is going to be 3D. They will follow the same path.

The downside of this strategy is that it can have a negative effect on purchase patterns. Savvy buyers often figure out what is happening and delay their purchase as a result. This can be mitigated two ways. The first is to maximize the time between price decreases so that there is a significant cost of waiting. The other way to mitigate buyers putting off a purchase is to strip features as you drop the price.

Penetration Pricing

Penetration pricing is expected to drive huge volumes of product into a market, taking a product or business from new and unknown to dominant at high velocity, penetrating broad and deep in the market.

Penetration pricing is driven by the belief that customers prefer lower prices. Logically it sounds true, and it can be; however if you have two products that the buyers know nothing about some will choose the low price while others choose the higher price. That is because some see less risk in the lower price and others see less risk in the higher price. A higher price holds the perception of quality. The old saying "you get what you pay for" has a strong influence on our psyche. If everyone preferred lowest price, there would only be Kohl's and no Neimann Marcus, there would only be drugstore sunglasses and no Bulgari, there would only be Yugo and no Rolls-Royce, there would only be Hanes and no *Carine Gilson*. The list goes on and on. Obviously, if everyone preferred the lowest price and shopped only based on price, the diversity that exists in the market would not be there. There would be no luxury offerings of any kind.

Apple manages big, fast penetration with a new product, yet practices skimming rather than penetration pricing.

The dangerous idea behind penetration pricing is that market share automatically equates to profit. This myth cropped up back in the late '60s and spawned a cult of thought. The concept has been hailed by many business leaders including Jack Welch who said GE would not participate in any category in which it did not hold either the number one or number the two positions in market-share. As a result a whole generation of businesses have been destroying margins in search for the holy grail of market share. It is believed you get there faster and surer with penetration pricing. Amazon has sold e-books at a loss in order to dominate the e-reader market with its Kindle, on the theory that its market share will equate to profit after the fact.

To be fair, there is some truth in the idea. The company with the greatest market share should enjoy economies of scale. That is, they should be able to produce their offerings for a lower price than their competitors. They may also kill off competitors early, avoiding costs of ongoing head-to-head competition. Dan Kennedy tells a story of once selling a company to its competitor for considerably more than it was intrinsically worth, based largely on the savings snared by the buyer by not having to compete with it going forward.

Being number one matters. But how you get to number one matters too. For most small businesses, profit must come before market share. If you prioritize growth over profit then you run a significant risk of never reaching profitability, and running out of gas before you get to the last lap, let alone the checkered flag and trophy. Market share is nice, profit is better, and often, the market-share leader never becomes the most profitable competitor in the field. Penetration pricing is not for the faint of heart nor the thinly capitalized.

While penetration prices are low in comparison to the rest of the market, that does not always mean they are cheap. The advent of Lexus was an example of this. The car company saw a gap between the average car market and the luxury market. They determined that they could pull buyers up, from basic to luxury, and pull luxury buyers down to more affordable product, creating a new category they would lead and dominate.

As you can see, there are many ways to work your way to the price you finally settle on and present to the marketplace, and you will likely wind up setting prices differently for different products and services, maybe for different markets, maybe at different times. Penetration pricing is a timing driven, typically short-lived price strategy replaced by others. Prices set by other methods may live long and produce great prosperity with only tweaks up or down based on costs, seasons or competitive influences. How

RESOURCE

There are 32 different pricing models, plus 7 advanced strategies to dramatically boost profits, featured in free information at www. SimplePricingSystem.com.

you set your prices is one of the most important decisions you make in business. It deserves a lot of thought.

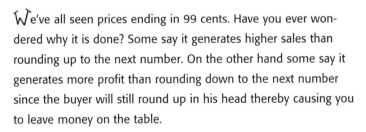

Where Did 99 Cents Come From?

Jason Marrs

We've all seen prices ending in 99 cents. Have you ever wondered why it is done? Some say it generates higher sales than rounding up to the next number. On the other hand some say it generates more profit than rounding down to the next number since the buyer will still round up in his head thereby causing you to leave money on the table.

The origin of 99 cents depends on who you ask. Paul Harvey said that it was created in Chicago by newspaper publisher Melville E. Stone who sold his paper for a penny. In order to generate more sales he talked newsstand operators into selling their products for a penny less than an even number so that buyers would be encouraged to spend the extra penny on his paper.

Another theory holds that it was done to fix a flaw in cash registers. Cash registers were seen as a great invention in 1883, and you have to credit it as such since they're still in use today. They allowed merchants to record and track every transaction except one, the one that never got entered. To solve the problem of unscrupulous cashiers pocketing money it is believed that merchants started ending their prices in 99 cents to force the cashier to use the cash register in order to make change.

Finally some believe that it was used by merchants to better track and identify sale-priced items. I frequent a wine store that does this. Their sale items all end in 7.

Regardless of where this all started, one of the big reasons it continues is because it works. For some strange reason more people will pay $9.99 than will pay $10.00. It is totally irrational but testing continues to prove it true. But it is not universally true. There are, of course, real psychological barriers in prices such as $20.00, $50.00, $100.00, and $500.00. So the idea of staying just below them has long proven to be a successful strategy in pricing. This all varies from business to business. I tend to use round numbers in my healthcare business. In my experience with that business and market, zeros work great. Of course we attract a very high-end market. My personal theory is that the odd numbers are seen as nickel-and-diming. I don't know the reason. I just know that it works well in that business at this point in time.

That said, I do currently have some new packaged products that I have developed for the business. While their total numbers are round, their discounted numbers all end in 7. I am testing different end numbers in these prices and, at this writing, have not yet determined whether 7, 9, or 0 serves me best. As with most things in business, the reality is that you need to test them. Just because 0's or 7's work great in one market for one offering does not necessarily mean they'll transfer over to another offering in a different market. Many swear that a 3 is the kiss of death while others swear that it is a godsend. You don't know for certain until you test.

CHAPTER 18

Why Not Charge People to Buy From You?

Dan Kennedy

Would you be interested in a fascinating "secret" about the rich vs. the poor?

Before you answer, let me share one of the 28 Wealth Magnets from my book *No. B.S. Wealth Attraction in The New Economy,* Magnet #24: Behavioral Congruency. In briefest form, this says that you can't reasonably expect to be wealthy unless you adopt the behavior of the wealthy that separate them from the non-wealthy and never-to-become wealthy. You can't reasonably expect to have an exceptionally prosperous business unless you utilize the practices that separate prosperous from poor and always-struggling businesses. This is behavioral congruency. Your behavior must be congruent with your ambitions, and the behavior of those successfully achieving your ambitions.

Now, would you like to know a fascinating "secret" about the rich vs. the poor?

The rich are paid for what they do in advance, before they do it. The poor are paid after their work. The poor work from the first through the fourteenth day to be finally paid on the fifteenth. The rich are paid before they even begin. Trump gets "points" in a real estate development and, often, upfront cash too, before the first brick is delivered to its site let alone laid, the developer gets his fee for assembling the investors before building begins, the architect gets a retainer before even writing one line on blueprints—but the bricklayer, he works from the first through the 14th day to be finally paid on the 15th. There are many practical reasons it is better to be paid before rather than after. There are remarkably powerful metaphysical reasons too. Because being paid before rather than after puts you squarely in the company of the rich instead of the poor, you *are* rich rather than poor. Mental state is precursor to physical reality.

So, why not add price strategy to your business that gets you paid before, by literally charging people fees of some kind merely for the privilege of subsequently buying goods and services from you? Get paid in advance and get paid for "air" too!

Can't be done? Really?

Country clubs do it. Night clubs have cover charges. Disney World does it: you are paying admission to enter a giant, interconnected web of souvenir shops surrounded by "attractions" that drive sales of the items in the stores. Racetracks do it: they charge for parking, admission, and programs, for you to have the privilege of wagering (on which they profit) and eating in their restaurants or at their concession stands. Hertz does it— their top-level #1 Club Membership carries a fee of $1,500.00 a year, for which you get to rent cars from them. I do it: new clients pay, as of this writing, $18,800.00 for an initial consulting day devoted, in large part, to determining what projects I'm going to do for them, for which they will pay fees and royalties. Many consultants and copywriters do those kinds of initial meetings free, in hope of securing assignments. Not me. No free lunch. I have guided clients of mine in the pizza business, other kinds of restaurants, retail stores, and professional practices to converting customers to members and collecting access fees.

This strategy delivers several benefits. First, it is a product with a price collected, before any other purchases are made, so that you at least get some money from each and every customer regardless of their subsequent purchase activity. This money can fund your advertising, marketing, and promotion, as well as provide profit. Second, the customer who pays for the right to buy is infinitely less likely to spread his purchasing around and buy elsewhere, and likely to patronize your business more frequently than he otherwise would. If you've paid $1,500.00 for the privilege of renting cars from Hertz, are you going to call Avis? We own a Disney time-share in Orlando. Owning it motivates (compels) us to vacation there, on average, two to three times more often each year than we would otherwise. It's a discouragement to go elsewhere and pay for lodging at a vacation destination when we already own one with annually expiring points at Disney. This brings us back to their souvenir, apparel and gift stores, and restaurants with greater frequency.

Another, related price strategy is membership with pre-purchased services, that may not be fully utilized, thus giving you the extra profit of "breakage" or non-redemption. You're most familiar with this in the fitness club industry. But if you'll visit KennedysBarberClubs.com you'll find an outstanding example of tiered levels of membership incorporating pre-purchased services, with a set monthly fee charged to the member's credit card on file. Some percentage of members do not utilize all they've paid for every month, and the non-fulfillment pushes the overall business' profit up. Of course, the members fully utilizing their pre-paid benefits are most likely to remain members for life, ascend from lower to higher level, and refer, so the breakage is a double-sided coin. But on one side, there is heightened profit. Keep in mind this concept is being done with *barber shops.* Not a country club with a golf course, bar, restaurant, or card room. A barber shop. Also, these members have access to buying proprietary products at the stores not included in monthly membership, so, they are paying for the privilege of buying.

There will be growing controversy over closed-door, membership based medical practices if anything close to the "Obamacare" legislation hustled through a see-no-evil Congress in 2010 actually gets implemented, because more and more MD's will convert from open-door to this model, freezing out Medicare and Medicaid patients and other insureds with poor coverage— to the point that you may have a little card that says you have health insurance, but you may find it damnably difficult to get health care. More like trying to redeem frequent flier miles than the current system. This trend has already been taking hold, but it may accelerate. The AMA and the federal government are both "critical" of concierge and closed-door, membership practices because they can see the writing on the wall of the trouble brewing, but unless and until the government passes law to tell doctors they must practice with doors open to all, more and more practices will be converted to these models.

The typical closed-door practice conversion looks like this: a letter goes out to, say, 4,000 patients who get care there, from frequently to periodically, telling them a switch to preferred, members' only care is occurring; describing benefits to members; and playing the scarcity card—that only 400 members will be accepted out of the 4,000 current patients. This the equal of having 10 people standing 50 feet from the stage, dragging but one stool on stage, and telling the 10 only one can get to sit on stage in the magic seat and have a chance to win a car. The 400 members may pay from $1,000.00 to as much as $5,000.00 per year for "exclusive" access to the doctor(s) and a collection of included services, such as regular exams, treatment of run-of-the-mill problems like colds, flu, etc., supervision of hospital care any time it is needed (but many other tests and treatment are extra, on a cafeteria menu—so the member-patients are paying for right to buy). At an average fee of just $2,000.00 times 400, the doctor has locked in $800,000.00 in revenue, a large portion paid in advance of any utilization, with none of that money subject to insurer interference, discounting or delayed reimbursement. The net profit in it, after costs of delivery of included services, will be substantially higher than the normal net profit from pay as you go and insurance billed services. Generally speaking, the doctor will have better, more compliant patients and a less stressful practice. As of this writing, there are approximately 5,000 concierge or membership medicine doctors in the United States, including those in the Pinnacle Care Health Advisory network. The number is expected to increase as much as 10-times in just two years, spurred, as I said, by doctors' disgust with Obamacare. I expect similar models to gain traction with dental, chiropractic, and other practices. *(Source: Wikipedia, Concierge Medicine, 7/2010.)*

This, incidentally, is not as new or unorthodox in other types of professional practices, notably accounting, financial services, and investment management, where retainers and annual fees have been around for quite some time.

So, let's assume you own a popular, always busy, and, on weekends, crazy-busy restaurant. You could offer a VIP Membership including guaranteed reservations on weekends requested as late as Thursday evenings, seating in a velvet-roped or glass-walled VIP section with service by the waiter of your choice guaranteed, and special members' only events—like wine tastings—for X-dollars a year, let's say $495.00, or with one pre-paid, all-inclusive dinner for two per month bundled in, at $2,000.00, available only to 100 people. At $495.00: $49,500.00 At $2,000.00: $200,000.00. Some or all, 100% net profit. Many years ago, when I lived in Phoenix, a popular night club and restaurant sold VIP cards for $500.00 that entitled you to bypass the line at the front door on weeknights and go right in, or go *to the shorter line* at the back door on weekends. I'm told they sold over 500 VIP cards—that's $250,000.00—and by the length of the shorter line some weekends, I don't doubt it. (I bought a VIP card.) Now let's translate that into price. Assume the customer comes twice a week, so 104 times a year. Sometimes just has a couple drinks, other times has dinner, averaging out to $50.00 per visit or $5,200.00 for the year—a very good customer, by the way. By charging him $500.00 for his entry, we essentially raised prices on him by 10%. If he comes less often and spends less, we may have raised prices on him by 20% or 30%. Without him ever thinking about it in that way. Price is seen every time a purchase made; membership fee seen only once a year or every two years if sold that way, or mostly unnoticed as an automatically recurring monthly charge to a credit card.

As you can now see, this is a price strategy—although neither merchants or consumers think of it as such.

CHAPTER 19

When Is Abusive
Pricing Smart?

Dan Kennedy

Y ou might think the answer to that question—when is *abusive pricing smart?*—is **never, but times are a'changin.** It seems to me that people are getting dumber and, in sync, much more easily abused. Everybody's pretty much accepted working without wages—pumping your own gas, making your own salad, checking out your own groceries. I fought the gas thing to the bitter end. I may grow my own food before doing self-checkout at the supermarket. Doing minimum wage jobs never appealed to me. Doing them free, as slave labor, appeals even less. Morons have let this be popularized as "convenience." Nonetheless, the concept has been popularized and is accepted in more and more venues. It is a price strategy, charging people for service not given.

One of the most amazing examples of this is at the car wash. The vacuuming out of the car used to be a service included with the wash 'n wax. Now it is not. Instead, you go to a vending machine with a vacuum cleaner attached, feed it dollar bills to buy minutes, and play beat the clock while doing your own vacuuming. The last place I was at, the automated wash 'n wax was $19.00. The vacuum cleaner, $1.00 for, I think, 4 minutes of suction. There are a couple dirty jokes there, but this is a business book for polite company, so I'll skip it. They're obvious, so entertain yourself without me. Be clear about it: the customer is paying for air and the privilege of providing his own service. At the other end of the wash tunnel, there are wipe guys, who dry the car off by hand. Will they soon be replaced by a paper towel vending machine?

Everybody's resigned themselves to extra charges on their hotel bills for drinking water (!) and newspapers. As I was writing this, American Airlines announced an $8.00 rental fee for blanket and pillow and a European airline installed pay toilets. Why not follow Lewis Black's idea? Rip out all the seats, hand each passenger a stick to jam up their butts and balance on . . . fit a lot more in the plane, save gas, reduce that nasty carbon footprint. Eventually, they could charge extra for the sticks. Or for lube.

Here's a new, cute gambit: I just filled out an order form from a catalog company that included this extra, check-off item: *"Health Services Fee: voluntary contribution to help defray the cost of medical insurance for our employees. Add $1.00."* I'll bet a lot of dummies contribute. I also, while writing this, got the first of, I imagine, many letters to come from several of my banks notifying of a new FDIC insurance fee to be paid, in response to their increased costs for FDIC insurance (something we are supposed to be getting from the government as taxpayers), and other new fees birthed by the banks' new compliance costs imbedded in

President Obama's financial industry reform. Maybe you've noticed: whenever he says "reform," he means "taxes."

This kind of nickel-and-diming and sneaky thievery used to annoy people, so it once was very bad business policy. Now I'm not so sure. Yes, it annoys *me*, but not enough to go through the hassle of closing those bank accounts and moving that money, and to where? Not enough *not* to drink a bottle of water, and I don't remember to punish that hotel chain on next trip, and, anyway, where would I stay where this rip-off hasn't been replicated?

I consider it abusive and you probably do too. But, to the extent customers will accept it and not hold a grudge, not doing it leaves money on the table.

This *can* be a clever way to reduce the price people focus on, and it's not new. The advertised price of the car doesn't include added tax, title, dealer prep, and delivery charges; shipping and handling gets added to the total catalog order after you've picked out your items—not to each item as you go.

Pregnant Question 1

To what extent can YOU get away with this, without damage—or with acceptable level of damage?

It has to be worth doing and aggravating some folks. An extra $3.25 from 10 customers a month, no. From 10,000, you betcha. I have a client who switched delivery of a very elaborate home study course to PDF, online without lowering its $495.00 price, added a "deluxe option" including a printed copy. i.e.. "library edition" delivered in a box for $200.00 more, and in 3 months testing, over 65% of the 300 or so buyers bit on the deluxe upsell, and overall conversions barely dipped a smidgen. Sheesh. He's charging a $200.00 premium for delivering what was standard as a deluxe option and nobody's batting an eyelash.

Question 2

Alternatively, can you make something of not doing this?

Southwest Airlines tried doing this in 2010, with its "bags fly free" campaign. All-inclusive resorts and cruise ships have this, but, in my opinion, don't promote it enough. As I discussed in the previous chapter, MD practices are excluding all Medicare and Medicaid patients (in skyrocketing numbers; average wait for Medicare patient to get an appointment has gone from 9 days in 2007 to 21 days in 2009, and I predict 60 days by 2012) and either going "concierge" (fee for access + fee for service) or "all-inclusive" (one set monthly fee covers anything + everything needed within a menu). Walt Disney originally re-invented the amusement park by eliminating tickets for each ride in favor of one admission = unlimited access to everything, then, in more recent years, brought forth the Express Pass (access to shorter lines) and the VIP Guides (to skip the lines) at premium prices, added attractions and extra park hours available only to its (pricey) resort guests, some only to concierge-floor guests. These are all examples of bucking the trend, and offering customers a simple, single price rather than a low price for something minimalist, then tacking on fees for this, that, and the other thing until the list of add-ons is as long as your arm. Is there any caché or competitive advantage in doing this and promoting that you are "all-inclusive" in your business?

Question 3

Can you get away with Disney's deal of being able to brag about an all-inclusive price, no nickel-and-diming, sneaky charges AND still pile on extra charges?

Yes, all the rides and attractions in the park are covered by the one price admission, but then the Express Pass or Guide and extra hours are, well, extra. It's an all-inclusive deal that isn't all-inclusive.

Abuse, of course, is strictly in the mind of the customer. Whether you view your own price strategy as abusive or not doesn't matter a lick. It's only the customer's attitude about it that matters.

In the direct marketing world, the little devil called "shipping and handling" is much manipulated. One legendary promoter of various kitchen gadgets via TV infomercials I'm not going to name has long lived by this price strategy: hard product cost plus actual shipping costs equals the shipping and handling fee charged the customer. So the entire selling price of the product goes only to the media cost of airing the show and his profit. This has been adopted with a slight twist by a number of gadget sellers using one-minute commercials, who offer an extra one free, then a third one or a related item free—you, quote, just pay *separate* shipping and handling. In truth, you're paying costs of goods and shipping and handling plus a profit to the advertiser. At minimum, virtually every advertiser, catalog house, or other marketer does mark up actual shipping and labor costs a little, to squeeze an extra buck or two out of each sale. If they're selling an item for $29.95, sales might fall at $33.95, but nobody balks at $9.00 vs. $5.00 shipping and handling, so the sought after $4.00 is plugged in there. A lot of mail-order companies also offer options on order forms or order pages at websites, such as Express Processing for an extra $1.00 or $2.00, and Insurance guaranteeing replacement of any goods damaged in shipment for another dollar or two or three. Almost all companies are actually self-insuring; damaged goods have to be replaced. And, in most cases, all orders are processed the same or next day, whether extra money is paid for express service or not.

Very recently, I called to re-order checks for one of my bank accounts. It was all done without speaking to a human, by punching in numbers. The last question requiring a response offered to ship the checks using Check-Protect Delivery for an additional fee. Of course, there is no such thing as Check-Protect Delivery. All orders are shipped the same way. The only difference is a decal that says "Check-Protect Delivery." Further, losses due to stolen checks are already covered by my account agreement at the bank, and again by my homeowner's insurance. This is an entirely bogus service I'm very sure a lot of people are saying yes to.

These added fees are pure profit. Is all of that or any of that abuse of the customer?

In the case of the bank, it seems so. But I don't have a firm opinion about it. And my opinion doesn't really matter. If the customer's okay with it, and happier paying a lower price for the product, and a higher price for shipping, and that sells the most product, then that's what we should present. Remember, it *is* your RESPONSIBILITY at the helm of a business to squeeze maximum profits from it. That's your job. To reinforce that, at the end of this chapter, I've reprinted pages 34–38 from my book *No B.S. Wealth Attraction in The New Economy* (which I urge reading in full, as companion to this one).

There are variations of this theme in other businesses. When I order theater tickets at the advertised per-seat price, I may discover there's also a ticket processing fee. A lawyer may quote an hourly fee, but not mention he rounds up when billing you for time on the phone, so a 12-minute call is billed at a quarter hour, a 46 minute call billed as an hour. If you begin scrutinizing your every purchase, bill, statement, and credit card statement like a sharp-eyed Scrooge, you may be amazed at how much of this stealth profiteering has crept into your life as a consumer.

Again, abuse is in the experience of the buyer. I am not going to go so far as to suggest you outright steal from customers by charging for nothing at all, although this is clearly a reality even with major, trusted institutions. But things like shipping and handling including profit mark-up are very grey and murky areas. There's room for debate about what is and isn't abuse. You must make the call. But you should at least consciously consider each and every opportunity to boost transaction value and profit without affecting what is perceived as "the price" or appearing to raise prices.

I recently had a conversation with the owner of several optometry practices, who had experimented with raising his fees for office visits and his prices for glasses, and gotten quite a bit of blowback from his mostly elderly patients. After letting the dust settle for several months, he imposed several new fees itemized on patients' bills but never mentioned: one, a "lab services fee" added underneath the price of lenses; another, a shipping and handling fee, also added underneath the price of lenses; and a one year warranty fee for replacement of damaged frames (which he did anyway). From this, no blowback and few questions. In total, this averages out to about a 7% price increase on glasses. To his exam fees, he added a "records maintenance and insurance documentation for reimbursement" fee of $7.00. That's added over $30,000.00 yearly of clear profit. As he said to me, "that doesn't sound like much until you calculate that I'll probably be in practice for at least another ten years, so it's $300,000.00, which pays off my mortgage."

Reprinted from
No B.S. Wealth Attraction in The New Economy

Wealth Magnet 4

Accepting Your Role and Responsibilities

Oh, you're an entrepreneur? Greedy bastard! Surely you know that's what some people think about you, say about you behind your back.

A successful entrepreneur drives down the street in his Rolls-Royce or builds his mansion. If not to his face, behind his back, many grumble about his greed. But if they hit the mega-millions lottery they might very well do the same things—most lottery winners do. It's not a moral objection to greed they're expressing. It's the sin of envy.

Too often, achievement, accomplishment, ambition is defined as greed.

Here's my clarification: greed is attempting to get something for nothing, to take without exchange.

Is getting the most money possible for the goods or services you deliver greed or intelligence? Is it greed or ambition? Are you a better person if you voluntarily get less money than you could for the goods or the services you deliver? No—in fact, you are derelict in your duty as business owner. You have a duty to yourself, your family, your investors or partners or shareholders, your lenders, your vendors, and your customers, and that responsibility is to attain the absolute highest and greatest profits possible, so you can stay in business successfully to honor every commitment to every one of these constituencies. To settle for anything less than the most is absolute dereliction of the responsibility of business ownership and leadership. To settle for anything less is to leave your business vulnerable, possibly fragile. And you should be fired.

Now, here's my question for you: What is your entrepreneurial responsibility? What is the entrepreneur's responsibility? What must you do in order to deserve and earn your place on the planet? Your success, prosperity, security, wealth?

A lot of people think your purpose, your responsibility in life is to provide jobs. You see that reflected in the communities that are busily trying to pass laws and, in some cases, communities and states suing companies to keep them from moving or closing; because their responsibility is to provide jobs to the community.

Is your responsibility to provide jobs? I hope you don't think so.

If providing jobs makes your business successful, if adding jobs makes it more successful, that's terrific. But if operating the business with fewer employees makes it more profitable, then it is your sworn responsibility as its captain to operate it with fewer employees.

A lot of people think your responsibility is to pay taxes.

Personally, I'd be a little happier with my gigantic income tax bill if the IRS sent me pictures, maybe of citizens of the foreign countries we support and of welfare recipients here in the United States; like when you send money to the starving orphans organization and you get the photograph and a letter once in a while about how they're doing. I think every taxpayer should get some of those and have people assigned to them. So for your money, you get a picture of 17 people in Iraq or Afghanistan or Gooblesedyburg where we're building roads and schools and providing food—which we do even for the populations of countries openly hostile to us, like North Korea—and of 4 welfare recipients and 1 retired guy, maybe from GM, so you can put photos of all the people you're supporting up on the refrigerator. And they should all have to write you notes every once in a while, to let you know how they're doing. I'd feel better. Wouldn't you?

You have a legal responsibility to pay the minimum taxes required of you.

But your responsibilities as entrepreneur do not include paying any more taxes than the minimum legally required of you. If you can arrange your business structure or affairs differently or relocate your business in order to pay fewer taxes, it is your sworn responsibility to do so.

Is it your responsibility to improve your customers' lives? No, it is not. Now, it's pretty smart to sell them things that, if they use them as you intended, will improve their lives. That's smart. But it's not your responsibility to see that it gets done. Nor should you lose any sleep over the customers who do not use what you sell them to improve their lives.

I had to come to grips with that in my businesses very early on, or I'd have had my wealth attraction severely suppressed. A lot of my wealth has been derived from writing and recording and publishing information products intended to help people better their attitudes, thinking, skills, businesses, and finances—just like this book. Frankly, the shrinkwrap never comes off a whole lot of what I sell. And you will kill yourself in my business if you worry about making them take off the shrinkwrap. The books never get read. The ideas never acted on. My clients very successfully sell perfectly good exercise equipment that gathers dust in buyers' garages, bottles of health-producing nutritional supplements that age unopened on closet shelves, business opportunities never worked on, heck, even vacation homes they rarely visit.

Should I feel guilty about the majority who pay their money but then never do anything with what they bought? Should I follow them home and refund their money? When I take a cruise, stay at a top-flight resort, or buy another racehorse, I give no thought to whether the money paying for it came to me from someone who used what they bought or from someone who has never ben-efited at all. That's not my responsibility. It is theirs.

My preference is for you to actually read this entire book and extract from it ideas you act on and derive benefit from, but frank-ly that preference is based at least as much, if not more, on my profit motive, rather than your profit. Readers who do act on ideas turn out to be much better long-term customers.

Earlier in this book I mentioned having had a client who builds and installs deluxe, premium-priced backyard sheds. If his cus-tomer puts the shed in his backyard and never moves the crap out of the garage into the shed, and still can't park the car in the garage—or, more probably, he moves all of the crap out of the garage, into the shed, and then restocks the garage with more crap and still can't park the car in the garage—should my client go out there and give him his money back?

Of course not. In fact, he should go out there and sell him a second shed. Sell him garbage removal service. Sell him a how-to-do-a-garage-sale kit. *Sell him something.*

The entrepreneur's responsibility is this: maximum profit and wealth to his shareholders. If you're the sole shareholder, that's you. Then your responsibility is just to play fair, not lie, cheat, or steal. Integrity for the entrepreneur is optimizing sales and profits and value in the business he captains.

Just as the boxer who pulls punches in a championship fight lacks integrity, just as the quarterback who does not thoroughly prepare for the Super Bowl game lacks integrity, just as the lawyer who does not thoroughly prepare for trial and do everything he can for his client lacks integrity, just as the doctor who operates hung over lacks integrity, the business owner who "pulls his punches" also lacks integrity.

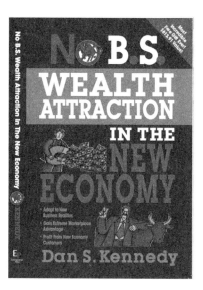

CHAPTER 20

Beware of Staff Sabotage
of Price Strategy

Jason Marrs

I magine head coach and quarterback agreed on an aggressive passing attack, but offensive coordinator and linemen committed to blocking schemes appropriate for a running game of three yards and cloud of dust, and the defensive coordinator and his players disgusted at the discord and dysfunction. How far will this *team* get? In working on the book, Dan Kennedy reminded me this actually happened—leading to defensive coach Buddy Ryan punching the team's offensive coordinator in the nose, on Monday Night Football, for all to see.

Most business owners or executives assume that their staff will implement their strategies like good soldiers. They forget that almost every army has suffered from "fragging"—grunts actually shooting their own generals in the back. We recently saw something not as violent, in the disagreement between the general in charge of the war in Afghanistan and the current Commander in Chief, played out in, of all places, the pages of *Rolling Stone* magazine. Assuming and relying on good soldiership is, like all assumptions, dangerous.

Considering its size, I have spent what could be called a god-awful sum of money in my backyard. Among other things we've removed a half a dozen trees, brought in one of those high-end custom built sheds that looks like a real house, and we replaced the existing chain link fence with a giant "privacy" fence. We also ripped out our side yard and upper patio to install two new patios that blend bluestone with two different kinds of high-end Cambridge pavers. You'd really be amazed at the difference between the before and after in our yard. I imagine we have spent more than all of the rest of our neighbors combined on their yards. And it shows.

Aside from being in my yard and an example of my blatant disregard for common sense, care to guess what all of these things have in common? In every single case the price was negotiated down without a single attempt at using value to stop the disappearance of profit. The first, last, and only answer to a price objection was to lower the price. This let us save thousands of dollars off the retail price while costing the business owners thousands of dollars in profit.

Other guys I know in the business have seen the work and were stunned at the low price I paid. They could not believe I got it for such a small sum. The patio is stunning. I am well aware that from a quality perspective it is worth more than I paid. And I would have cheerfully paid more. I didn't purely because I didn't have to. The company who installed it could have collected more profit had they taken the time and energy to use value selling. This happens all the time: the customer who would cheerfully have paid more, paying less.

They didn't get the price from me that I would have willingly paid because, in their minds, low price was the only tool they had to close the sale. They so feared losing a sale because of price, they negotiated privately with themselves, and came in low. Instead of really selling value, they took the approach requiring little thought or skill and sold on price. This is the sad reality of most business owners, but definitely most salespeople. They will throw away the business' profit easily, anytime there's opportunity to do so. If you depend on your sales staff to safeguard your profits on their own, you're doomed.

As a consumer, I confess, sometimes I make a sport of this, but I usually don't. It is just too time consuming to negotiate or price shop. When I walk through a grocery store I have absolutely no concept of the prices I'm paying. I don't look. Same goes with a lot of my shopping. I am there to buy what I want and get out. Just tell me what I owe you so I can get back to doing things that need to be done. Still, that doesn't stop countless employees on countless occasions giving me deals that I did not ask for and did nothing to deserve. One store I go to on occasion has a few checkers that pull out coupons from their aprons or pockets and scan them to save me money. Never mind that I didn't know the coupon existed and was ready to hand them money for the full price. There is the garden store where I go to buy flowers for our yard that has a checker who gives a significant "cute girl" discount for my daughter. There have been countless bartenders feeding me free drinks and waitresses discounting my tab. There is any manner of discounts, freebees, and bonuses that are given to me for no reason at all. I'd like to think that this is all because of my dashing good looks, but the bags under my eyes and the bulge in my belly tell me otherwise. Don't get me wrong, I enjoy them, but the gratuitous discounts given me by these employees are not helping the businesses they work for. And it is wrong to assume I'm the only guy who has such good luck. I'm not. This happens to a lot of people and it only represents a few of the ways employees sabotage your success by stealing your profit.

You might think that these are disgruntled employees. Occasionally that is true. However, in most cases it is not. Their people are not trying to hurt their employers. It is far more likely that they actually think they are helping and doing the right thing. In other words, not only do they not know that what they are doing is wrong, they think it is right. Often, the staff feels the prices you're charging are too high, so discounting if they can, or giving away free goods seems fair, just, and appropriate to them.

This is such a common occurrence I have to wonder if anyone actually takes the time to teach their employees where their paychecks come from. Not everyone understands business. In fact very few people do. It is one of my reoccurring complaints with our school system. Business needs to be taught and not demonized. Commerce is the root of society. Everyone is a part of it. It does not matter if you are the employee or the boss, professor or CEO, if you are being paid you are in business and you depend on a profit being made *somewhere*. Even the government can't survive without someone making a profit. If they continue to shackle businesses with burdens that cannot be met, we all suffer the damage. Profit is necessary, not evil. Society cannot survive or progress without it. As the boss it is your responsibility to make sure your employees understand all that. They can't get paid if there is no profit, and every cent they give away affects your profit and their ability to get paid. They need to understand this. You may even find that this is something you need to show them specifically. You may need to show them exactly what a buyer is worth, what all the costs of obtaining a customer are.

Try this experiment: ask each employee to write out a list of what they understand to be their ten most important responsibilities on the job. You'll discover very few if any of your staff members include "protecting and maximizing profits" or, for that matter, "preserving price integrity" or "implementing my boss' price strategy" on that list. There's no understanding of any of this, so there is bound to be both unintentional and intentional sabotage.

Your employees also need to understand how those you serve profit from buying your goods and services, and if your price strategy is focused around premium prices, how paying premium prices benefits the consumer. When someone is selling on price alone they do so because they do not realize that the buyer is actually making a profit. They assume that the seller is the only one making a profit. This is absolutely false. If the buyer does not believe that they will profit, they will not purchase. To take that a step further, the buyer will not purchase again if they do not believe that they made a profit the first time and will again this time. That is a fact. For the consumer, of course, "profit" may not be financial. It may be superior service, product reliability, a better environment, even better staff to serve them. These things all cost money and must be reflected in price, but employees who have not thought about this and are aware of other businesses in your category selling at prices lower than yours may simply think your prices are too high.

How your staff thinks about price and profit will greatly influence their attitudes and behavior, and either discourage or encourage unintentional and intentional sabotage by salespeople and other staff members of your price strategy. Given good education about this, any staff members still not on the same page and caught engaging in any sabotage—from undermining your authority and strategy with fellow staff members to failing to sell on value to theft, in form of unauthorized discounting or gifting—must go. For a lot more about these management issues, I recommend Chapters 5, 6, 7, 9, 13, 14, 15, 16, 21, 22, and 41 of

Dan's book in this series, *No B.S. Ruthless Management of People and Profits.*

Break the Negotiating Addiction

There is a big difference between knowing what a problem is and stopping the behavior. Selling on price is no different. Selling on price is like an addiction. Knowing the cold hard truth about profit may not be enough to prevent a relapse. You're going to have to break the negotiating habit cold turkey. You are not going to be able to allow deviation from your set prices. You can have different prices that represent different levels of value; however there is absolutely no reason to strip away profit. In short, price strategy as well as sales strategy must be strictly enforced.

It is not enough to say that you are the only person who can approve a discount. If you do this then what do you think will happen? You will quickly become acquainted with the law of unintended consequences. While you may have a brief reprieve from negotiating or unauthorized discounting, you will ultimately end up with a constant barrage of requests for discounts. Your job title will suddenly need to be changed from "boss" to "discounter-in-chief."

This is why you should start by getting rid of negotiating altogether. It is one thing if you want to have specific rules for how different customers secure different prices; it is altogether different to allow random discounts through negotiating. The only way to break the negotiating habit is to go cold-turkey. This is the only way you can force your staff to sell on value. If they have the option to discount they will, always.

This is going to be tough, if you've been "loose" about it. In fact, if you have a sales staff there are good odds there will be crying and complaining on a level that will remind you of watching a middle aged meth addict on an episode of the reality show *Intervention* telling his family all the reasons why they should continue enabling him. Still you must be strong if you want to get your profitability back and want to protect it. This is not a time to be weak. It does not matter how good your pricing strategy is if your staff undermines what you are doing.

While you're breaking the negotiating habit another step you need to take is shifting the commissions or bonuses you pay from gross to net. I bet you've never thought about that have you? That's okay, most businesses don't. In fact I've yet to talk to a business owner that did before consulting with me. Yet it's such a common sense move if you think about it. When would you expect an employee to have more incentive to protect your profit, when they get paid on the gross, or on the net?

When you pay them on gross it is possible for you to take a loss while they still profit. Don't laugh, you'd be surprised how often this happens. I did it myself at one point. It happened because costs crept up and I wasn't paying enough attention to the net on components of a bundled offering. There it was being pushed as part of a package and, concealed within the bundled price, it was being sold for less than cost. Of course, commission was being paid on the gross sales, and they looked very good.

If you have any salesperson who, after being educated about price and profit, and trained on value-based selling rather than selling on price, continues to negotiate away your profit or continues whining, complaining, blaming poor performance on your price strategy, badgering you about your strategy, or poisoning the attitudes of others on your team—they've got to go.

The Easiest Way to Protect Price and Profit Strategy Is . . .

That said, the easiest way to keep staff from screwing up prices and profits is to take it out of their hands. This can even be true about you, the owner. If you are making all the sales, you may be the staff person who needs to be removed from the process! The problem with you doing the selling is that if you have already been discounting, then you will have a hard time saying no, especially with spoiled clients. The human variable is a big one, because we have empathy and compassion, fear and anxiety, bad habits. Process has none of these foibles, so the more of your selling is done by process, the better.

What does process in place of people actually mean? Some businesses can convert altogether, with customers buying online or from marketing materials with fixed prices presented and no opportunity of attempting to negotiate. Some businesses do a better job of convincing people that prices are fixed than others: people generally accept menu prices in restaurants but nobody gives any credence to a car dealer's posted or advertised price. For a time, GM's separate brand, Saturn, seemed to be making some headway in restoring belief in a sticker price, but they lacked the will to stick with it and enforce it with dealers and their salespeople. At bare minimum, you can design a marketing process that weeds out tire-kickers and committed price buyers before they even get face to face with you or your salespeople, moving much of the selling forward into the advertising, websites, online video, and literature they go through before arriving at a sales event, and that builds value, exclusivity, scarcity, expertise, and authority for you and your product in the buyer's mind before that sales event. This is the kind of marketing methods that my friends at Glazer-Kennedy Insider's Circle™ are so ingenious and effective at guiding people to, in hundreds of different kinds of businesses, which is good reason to accept their invitation on page 234.

Although moving toward process in place of people is an admirable aspiration, I'm sorry to say that most businesses will never fully escape the human variable; the owner, sales representative, sales clerk, waitperson, service technician being face to face with a customer or prospective customer and presenting price and responding to push-back.

Get on Board or Get Out

Ultimately, you cannot protect your price strategy or your profits without training, ongoing coaching, smart incentives, *and firing*.

As a result of reading this book, you are going to want to make changes throughout your business, but particularly with respect to price strategy. When change happens there is usually someone who refuses to get on board. There is only one answer to this person, and it is simple. Get on board or get out. If you have staff that won't get on board with the program, they have to go NOW. I am a firm believer in this. The old saying is true: one bad apple *will* spoil the whole damn bunch. You cannot afford to be unduly tolerant or patient.

How do you know who the rotten apple is? The most likely candidate will be someone who has depended heavily on discounting in order to make sales. It could even be the person you thought was your rockstar salesperson. He represents a real danger to you when you take away or rein in use of the tool he has been relying on to eat. You'll have to be out on the floor, on the alert. Where, when, and from whom are you hearing or over-hearing grumbling? Who is having the most difficulty making the transition? Who is blatantly disobeying your orders or pushing customer complaints up to you?

Some people just don't have the right mindset to sell at premium prices, or even at fixed prices. Some people resent affluent customers, some do not believe customers who buy based on factors other than price even exist, some are not willing to work harder to make sales at higher, fixed prices, even if it

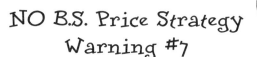

NO B.S. Price Strategy
Warning #7

**Any idiot can come up with a long list of reasons why
he can't implement and enforce the best possible strategies
in his business.** That kind of thinking isn't even worth paying
minimum wage for. "But MY Business Is Different!" is the
rallying cry of the poor. Creative adaptation is the behavior
of the rich. If your reaction to the Chapters to this point has
been to quickly invalidate much as things YOU can't do in
YOUR business, stop here, return to the beginning, and start
over. This is especially true of Price Strategy. The business
owner who clings to past Strategy FOR ANY REASON
lets his past determine his future.

benefits them financially to do so. There are lots of reasons that
someone may be a happy staffperson or productive salesperson
in one place but a constant complainer, trouble-maker, or failure
in another. You have to keep an eye out for problem people in
your place and deal with them as quickly as possible.

I once had a woman who came highly recommended to our
company. Her background and her references looked fantastic.
We let her get into a position that was important to one of our
programs. Unfortunately she was shocked by the price we were
selling a certain service for. She could not get her head around
the idea that it was actually a good thing. We tried everything.
We talked about the costs to run the program. We talked about

the income level of the clientele. We talked in-depth about the fact that high prices are a good thing because they support exceptional service and actually help to develop newer and better products and services. We even tried having her read high-end magazines such as *ROBB Report* in an effort to expand her mind to the reality of just how much money exists. After a period of time she play-acted like she got it. Still, my better judgment told me she was not committed. She wasn't. Aside from the damage she caused while with us, she eventually walked out on the company without notice, leaving us scrambling to fill the void. Better I should have sent her packing earlier. When a member of your staff is a problem, they have to get on board or get out. If not, it will cost you much more to keep them than it will to let them go. It's better to cut your losses than to let them magnify.

Price integrity and profitability in a business are very fragile assets. They are unable to protect themselves. They need a big, strong, resolute defender. That defender has to be you.

CHAPTER 21

A Jury of Four
But Only One Decides Fate

Dan Kennedy

T here are four jurors of your prices and price strategy:
  1. You
  2. Your Staff, Associates, Family, and Friends
 3. Your Peers
 4. Your Customers

Only one of these jurors has any right to rule your fate.

#2. Your staff, associates, family, and friends all have many reactions, thoughts, feelings, and opinions about your prices. Most think they are too high—or worse, unfair, unreasonable, predatory, or stupid—regardless of how low they may be. Lowering them to curry favorable opinions from these folks is futile and foolish. These negative and critical opinions link to

four things you should live so long as to alter: one, a generally held negative opinion of all business owners and sellers; two, a generally held negative opinion, resentment, and envy of the self-employed, the successful, and the rich; three, a generally held negative opinion of the prices of anything and everything; and four, a complete ignorance or misunderstanding of economics, free enterprise, business, costs of doing business, and virtually everything in this book.

Cartoon reprinted from advertising for Dan's book *No B.S. Wealth Attraction in The New Economy*.

I can assure you, if you hand the pricing gun and supply of blank price stickers over to anybody on this list, they will set your prices lower than even you would have set them before reading this book. For that reason, you dare not hand over the *emotional* pricing gun either. They cannot be permitted influence on your price strategy, prices, or your own thoughts and feelings about them. Whatever "stuff" of theirs that you invite or allow into your thoughts will pollute or poison, not enrich and nourish.

There may be instances where you feel it's advisable to *pretend* to welcome and consider their input on these matters. But never take any of it seriously.

#3. *Your competitors, your business neighbors, your peers* in your industry, peers who are members of the same trade association, and maybe some grand pooh-bahs of your industry or its association also have many reactions, thoughts, feelings, and opinions about your prices. Most think they are too high—or worse, unfair, unreasonable, predatory, or stupid—regardless of how low they may be. Lowering them to curry favorable opinions from these folks is futile and foolish. You might mitigate envy and resentment with acquiescence, but then again you might not, and anyway, really, is the approval of people who make no actual contribution to your success or security so important? Some of these critics can be very vocal, some can be bullies. Know that the louder they screech or the more they bully, the more envious and resentful they are. Their secret disappointment with their own finances is acted out in disapproval of you, your business practices, and your success. I can assure you that Jason and his wife are, to their faces and behind their backs, talked about as *pirates*, by all those working for wages in government bureaucracies and all the other therapists in private practices barely making a living. I have been characterized this way by peers in every profession and business I've been or am involved in—professional speaking, consulting, direct-response copywriting, and with my information products, trainings, and seminars. I fly the pirate flag happily. Tongue in cheek, I even used the pirate theme for a seminar of mine called Wealth Days—we showed pirate movies, gave everybody skull-and-cross bones goodie bags and pirate hats, had a big cardboard pirate ship in the room for photos, and decorated with pirate flags.

The only real way to be well-accepted and popular with peers is to be pitiable, to be poorer than they are.

#1. *You*. Your thoughts and feeling about your price strategy and, in broader sense, about money, prosperity, and wealth matter a great deal. Since you *are* writing your own paycheck *as you price*, your thoughts *are* essentially your bank balance. This is why philosophy matters and can't be separated from the practical aspects of business success. But even you don't have real power here.

#4. *The only juror with real power over your destiny*. The customer. It is how *he* reacts, thinks, and feels about your pricing that determines whether the paycheck you wrote for yourself clears the bank or bounces back, marked NSF in nasty red letters. If he reacts positively and every friend and relative and peer and staff-person you have reacts negatively, you will be financially victorious. If friends, family, peers, and employees were ever to react positively to your pricing (and your success)—an unlikely miracle—but the customer reacts negatively, you will be poor.

There is, of course, great responsibility on you to present self and products and services and prices in the best manner possible, to the best qualified customers obtainable, in order to successfully sell at the highest prices and profits possible. That's not the customer's responsibility at all. It's all yours. But then he is the lone juror with legitimate clout.

Too much attention given to the judgments of the jurors with no legitimate clout is how people undermine their own ambition and achievement.

CHAPTER 22

Price in
Recessions

Dan Kennedy

The fear-based, panic-driven, wimp-embraced price strategy of the recent recession has been to drop prices as far as they could be dropped, and by necessity, drop quality, service, and customer experience right along with it.

This flies in the face of one of the great, universal truths about price: that the overwhelming majority of buyers of any product(s) or service(s) prefer making their choices based on criteria other than lower price, and will do so, and spend more than the cheapest available price and/or more than originally intended *when given a good reason/value proposition and sufficient emotional motivation to do so*. This changes only slightly during tough economic times. If the combination of chronic, cyclical, and incidental unemployment runs 4% in good times and hits 12% in bad times, that's still only another 8% of consumers who may be so severely challenged financially that they deviate from their normal buying behaviors. Walmart reported getting customers through their doors in very recent years for the first time who have been "trading down" in response to the recession, loss of one of the two incomes in the household, investment losses or, absent need, a frugality impulse prompted by daily bombardment by the news media about the horrors of the recession. However, to Walmart's frustration, most of these customers are picking up savings on basics—paper towels and cleaning supplies, big bags of chips, and pet food—but still buying most everything else somewhere else. Of course, Walmart is already in the lowest-prices, high-volume business. Other merchants, service providers, and B2B vendors who stampeded in fear toward cheapest price territory did not necessarily find it to be higher, safer ground. Many left their profit margins behind without gaining volume or even maintaining accustomed volume, and actually made their circumstances worse.

The fact is, the overwhelming majority of consumers continue to buy most of what they buy and patronize most of the businesses they patronize despite price or cheaper prices offered elsewhere, with their choices based on criteria other than price, regardless of ups or downs in the economy. As example, a recent survey by the IBM Institute for Business Value found that in this recent recession, 72% of shoppers at grocery stores said that the quality of the products was more important than price; 68% said nutrition was their most important consideration. Of course, such claims are suspect, as people would think these are the "right answers." But the reality is close: consumer behavior tracked by the grocery industry indicated only about 50% of shoppers have been buying smaller amounts at a time and shopping at more than one store, to find the lowest prices (up from about 35% in 2006–2007), and 35% have been buying lesser brands or generics in some categories (up by about 7% from '06–'07 levels). However, more than 50% of shoppers armed with coupons let some coupons go unused and bought other, better brands. Get that. They clip coupons, they come with those coupons, yet they buy a different brand and let the coupon go unused. Number one reason given in survey for choosing a higher priced product: "it's better for my family." The percentage that are still willing to pay more for name brands vs. generics and/or more convenient packaging is 81%. Most significant, from a "marketing to the affluent" standpoint: premium brands and premium-priced specialty foods' sales remained steady during the recession. All this, mostly with commodities, with no salesperson involved. My take on all that data and information is that some consumers always buy cheapest price; some trade down under pressure, usually absent effective persuasion; but many "stay strong" buying by criteria other than price, and by preference or "mission" (e.g., providing best meals for my family). *(Sources: Grocery Shopping Survey by Synovate.com; Paying More for Brands & Packaging in a Recession—Report by Consumer Network @ epmcom.com; IBM Institute for Business Value, ibm.com/ iibv.)*

Even under adverse economic pressure, the majority of buyers respond to motivating factors others than price. They will even abandon their predetermined intent to buy at the cheapest price if given other persuasive criteria for their purchasing decision.

There is even a step up to better quality—and higher per item/ per experience prices - that occurs in recessions. Smart marketers can capitalize on upscale consumers' tendency in recession to cut back on the quantity/frequency of purchases while searching for best quality when they do purchase. For example, in '09, New Yorkers dined out 3 times a week vs. 3.3 times in '08, but their average dinner tab went UP 2.5% from '08, to $42.00 per person

(Source: Zagat). New York City is, incidentally, the second most expensive city to patronize restaurants in, behind London in the United Kingdom. And there was that pesky Wall Street crash, wiping out Bear Stearns, shrinking Goldman, emptying office suites. Net result: customers dialed back frequency a bit, but then went to slightly better (more expensive) places or splurged on extras to give themselves better experiences as exchange for their "sacrifices." Nationwide, mid-range chains wound up with disappointing results from price-cutting and advertising deeply discounted, 2 for 1, and low-price "bundle" (2 entrees, 1 appetizer, 1 dessert to share for just $15.00) offers. Many reported no increase or even losses in numbers of customers, but drops in per person spending, and bigger drops in profits. These customers still cut back on frequency but, since it was pushed on them, also took advantage of the low-price offers, and spent less per outing.

The path to prosperity in generally unprosperous times is rarely price cutting. No more sane than reacting to bleeding profusely from an attacker's knife wound by stabbing yourself in another place on your body.

To the befuddlement of most, there are also, always, businesses that score sales and profit increases in purportedly bad economic times, and do so without compromising their prices. Family-owned Skinner Baking Co. in Omaha saw sales rise 18% from '07 to '08. In December, 2008, a big 25% jump. Its ovens had to run 6 days a week vs. 5 before and they were hiring (!) to keep up with demand. They supply coffeecakes, cinnamon buns, etc. to supermarkets. They've been in biz since 1911, so their V.P. thinks he understands why their sales went up: "This is comfort food." The owner of Bathroom Magic in Fairfax, Virgina, reported '08 revenues up 75% vs. '07, and '08 being the best year he's ever had. Why? People who, in boom times, would bring in contractors to completely re-model their bathrooms, in these times chose a service they would otherwise sneer at: the one-day bath makeover, with refinishing glaze and fit-over components to re-finish a tub like new for just $425.00. The economy let him attract mass-affluent and even affluent customers. "When the economy goes down, my business skyrockets," he says. Interstate Batteries opened 43 new stores in '08—hiring to staff them, on top of the existing 125, and expanded the variety of batteries carried, although they're known for car batteries. "October and December, 2008 were the best months in the company's history," reported the president of this 56-year old company. Why? "With the recession, whether it's cars or laptops, people are keeping what they own and trying to extend the life of their products." *(Source: USA TODAY 2/2/09)*

OK, go ahead and get it out: *your* business is different. *Your* business isn't designed to get a boost from the recession. Duh! You can fix that. *Any* restaurant can create comfort food menus, comfort food nights. And since more people are staying home to eat, expand pre-prepared meal offerings—didja notice Pizza Hut's started advertising gigundo trays of lasagna? *Any* remodeler, contractor, furniture seller could reach up to more affluent customers than he normally attracts with value packages. *Any* retailer can alter or expand his product line to support a message right for these times. The question is not: how can I excuse myself from business modification so I keep my excuses for suffering? Not: how can I *survive* the recession? **The question is**: how can I be nimble, agile, creative, modify my business, alter my marketing to get a boost from recession?

The best recession or tough times price strategy is creative and complex—not a red pen to mark down prices.

As I am writing this book, the recession begun under Bush and dramatically worsened by Obama's wasteful spending spree, debt multiplication, and a massive assault on the private sector that has grown quite stubborn. Movement from it to a New Economy, as happens out the back door of every recession, is slow. You may now, still, be doing battle with business capital on strike and consumer hoarding of cash, with high unemployment, right along with one of the certain main ingredients of the evolving New Economy: more thoughtful, prudent, and knowingly empowered consumers. And/or the inevitable wave of sky-high inflation that must follow the dizzying debt accumulation of 2009 and 2010 may have arrived. (If not, it will.) When I write my monthly newsletters,* weekly memos,* and blogs,* I can be timely. The nature of book publishing requires 6 to 8 months lead time, sometimes more, so being precisely matched to present conditions on the ground or accurately forecasting is tricky. But what I can state with certainty is, whatever the specifics of the economy swirling around you, short of a repeat of 1929 and the '30s, your best price strategy will be in concert with smart marketing strategy, and it will not be accomplished simply with a bloody axe. Bring a full toolbox.

One thing that must be in that toolbox is superior sales process, people, and salesmanship. Price is supported by skillful selling; undermined by the absence of salesmanship. And absent it has largely been!

In 2009, on my major Christmas shopping day, I went to the large, upscale mall. I first bought myself a new suit at Nordstroms and had it tailored immediately, while I shopped, so I was there twice, once to buy, the other to pick it up. The pleasant, professional salesman made only a half-hearted reference to

---

*Glazer-Kennedy Insider's Circle™ Members have access to my most current thinking through the monthly *No B.S. Marketing Letter,* separate *No B.S. Marketing to the Affluent Letter,* other newsletters, monthly audio programs, weekly memos, and members-only online resources. Information is in this book, page 234.

overcoats on sale, but no attempt to offer a second suit at a discount or show me sports jackets, trousers, anything else. I paid $950.00 for the suit. *I guess that was all he wanted.* Downstairs, I got my boots shined, sitting facing the men's shoe department, wearing obviously expensive boots. Two salesmen stood idly by; neither came over, introduced himself, complimented me on my boots, offered a business card, wondered aloud if I might have interest in any new footwear. I wonder if the musings they were so occupied by had to do with how bad business was—*or perhaps they had made all the money they wanted for the year.*

At the Brighton store, I bought a women's bag and two gift certificates, one for $200.00, the other for $100.00. When asked if they were for different people, I said "Of course—one for my wife, one for my mistress. Care to guess which is for which?" I did it to bedevil the rather annoying woman customer next to me hogging all the counter space, which I succeeded at. But from the two "salespeople" required to ring my sale—including having to look the bag up in their catalog because the register wouldn't accept the code on the tag—no attempt at selling me anything else . . . even though the catalog page had two other items that matched the bag I was buying. *Maybe they were idle rich ladies, just working in the store for fun.*

At Saks, at the Chanel counter, I had only the name of the skin care line, no particular products in mind. After determining I did not know exactly what I wanted, with a small sigh and a muttered "of course, you wouldn't know that," she did no selling of products; asked me the amount I wanted to spend; built and boxed a package. About $400.00. It so happens I know more about cosmetics and skin care than you'd guess, so I happen to know there were three little jars displayed there, *each* priced above $500.00, but she made no attempt to sell them. She accepted the $400.00 number I gave her; she gave me no information or incentive to up my number, and damn if I was going to do her work for her. *After all, she must be quite content with her income as-is, so why should I trouble her with more?*

At the nearly empty American Greetings store, on entry I walked past three clerks yakking with each other; on exit, 10 minutes later passed the same yakking clerks. At the Papyrus store, a clerk actually made attempts at being helpful and at upselling. Meager and ineffectual attempts but attempts nonetheless. At the Godiva store, I naturally picked the big basket with Christmas assortment of goodies they only had one of; waited while a sadly dimwitted clerk was sent to the storage room to find a second only to return to say they had none. I wanted two, they were $175.00 each. Rather than offering to assemble the second one from its individual items all there in the store, my "salesperson" down-sold me to two $100.00 packages and when I grumbled that they weren't as Christmasy in appearance (brown instead of red ribbon, etc.), she just shrugged. I also bought seven small packages of imported truffles; no attempt to upsell me to the larger collections. I got a $40.00 gift card as "bonus," thrown into my bag with bare comment.

At the independent bookstore, usually pretty well-run, I stacked up and ultimately bought $400.00 worth of books plus $100.00 in gift cards. The fellow had trouble loading the gift cards, which he clearly found irritating, and made no comment about any of the books being purchased—like: "if you like this author, you'd really like so-and-so" . . . or: "is this collection of great Cleveland Browns games DVD's a gift? We have autographed books by Browns players in the sports section." His only comment was: "You're sure buying a lot of books." At their in-store coffee shop, I stood for over 5 minutes at the "Please Wait To Be Seated" sign while the person who was supposed to seat me stood at the back talking with another employee, so I seated myself, then went over and started getting myself a cup of coffee, which did get her attention—but I wasn't offered a fresh baked scone. Much later, at

Starbucks, buying gift cards, their gift packages of coffees were not mentioned. Incidentally, the *New York Times* that day ran an article about all the New York publishing companies laying off staff—even *editors*, oh horror of horrors; delaying new book releases, freezing acquisitions; the CEO of Barnes & Noble saying this is "the worst retail environment he's ever seen"—I would say, more accurately, it's the pee-poorest selling I've ever seen. Environment schmironment. Finally, on the way home, I stopped by a local restaurant to get a take-out order, sat at the bar, listened to the owner tell me about how their group party business was off and, generally, dinner business soft. I wasn't offered a special on gift certificates. I say: nuts to 'em all. But: **is this going on in YOUR business?** Worse, are YOU personally guilty—of not selling?

Theories About the Death of Salesmanship

This paucity of salesmanship hasn't repaired itself since that outing. Pretty much everywhere I go, I note the absence of good sales process, and lack of initiative and effort from staff to sell. This reflects not just on salespeople and other employees, but on managers and owners as well. I have five theories about the reasons for this strange phenomenon of non-selling:

1. *Assumption that nobody's buying, so why waste energy selling?* (Hibernation without even retreating to the cave.)
2. *Absence of know-how, skill, or even idea that they're supposed to be selling*—since people have been so freely spending and buying for so long on their own, despite pitifully poor salesmanship. (Ignorance.)
3. *Sloth.*
4. *Resentment of having to work.*
5. *With staff:* little, inconsistent, ineffectual training and/or supervision/enforcement; not enough fast firing of losers; insufficient incentive and reward for winners.

All these not only retard sales volume, they drive price reductions. The corporate or managerial response to a sales slump is almost always to cut prices, increase discounts, create deeply discounted "value specials." In 2009, Burger King franchise owners had to threaten to sue their parent company, to put a stop to its forcing bare-bones priced "value sandwiches" on them, on which they actually lost money, their profit then found only in side items and drinks. Please, don't be that dumb and feckless.

Instead, take a look at the five evils named above, and work on them—with yourself and with your staff. And please, quickly fire anybody who clings to any of these and replace them with the next batter up, repeatedly as needed, until you get somebody who really wants to play the game to win.

SECTION II

SAMPLES

CHAPTER 23

Sample Advertising
and Marketing Materials

From Jason and Isa Marrs' Practice
and the Price Strategy and Price Strategy Support Lessons
They Illustrate

1. **". . . That Few Parents or Therapists Know About."** Jason calls this their "Theory of the Mind" ad. This is a very effective ad that tends to attract a very serious, thoughtful parent, i.e. one for whom price of services or access to free services will be less important than a unique, superior approach to treatment. The ad lays the groundwork for differentiation between their practice and all other therapists. This translates to any business. The key ideas are (a) differentiation from competition, and (b) deliberately attracting potential customers for whom price will not be the driving factor of their buying decision. It also will repel less-qualified prospects, who may not be willing to take the time to read this much copy or are immediately looking for price information.

2. Right Decision Guarantee. This is use of a technique called 'risk elimination' or 'risk reversal' that is often especially important when selling at premium prices or fees AND selling something for which efficacy or satisfaction cannot be immediately determined. The risk imbedded in purchase goes up with price, so guarantees that provide adequate time to judge the outcome or satisfaction are needed to bring that risk down to match or trump the lower risk imbedded in a much lower price. In other words, if I pay $50.00 for something vs. $500.00, my risk is 1/10th as much at $50.00 and 10X as much at $500.00. To take the risk disadvantage out of the 10X price, I need a guarantee that is effectively 10X better. (This copy taken from their website.)

3. Good-Better-Best Offers Order Form. This Form shows how Jason has used tiered pricing and assembled three different packages or bundles of services. As we've said throughout this book, there is a customer for every price. Good-Better-Best options allow different customers to do their price shopping within the walls of your offerings, and make their decision in the context of "which is right for me?" (or: which can I afford?) rather than a simple yes/no. This is a powerful Price Strategy in and of itself, but it is plus-ed here by also presenting ala carte pricing, which is substantially higher than the same services bundled. This provides price comparison within the walls. It also gives the buyer a feeling of having gotten a bargain by choosing one of the bundles. It should be noted that this is not just handed out with a brochure; it is given to the parent only after a diagnostic process and recommendations are made.

4. Kids' Health Spectator. This is the FREE that Jason uses universally; past and present clients and prospective clients who opt-in free, online, or through advertising, receive this promotional and informational newsletter monthly. Giving this FREE in no way de-values any services or products that are being sold. Each issue has the same basic component parts: a seasonal or topical front-page article, a different condition-specific article about a particular child development problem, recognition of clients who've referred (providing reminder and reassuring evidence that clients refer), positioning of Isa Marrs, and direction to websites for more information. As you can see, this is an information-heavy approach, with the purpose described above in #1 in mind.

To see more, visit www.WhereICanBeMe.com and SpeechLanguageFeeding.com.

A Core Deficit Of Autism That Few Parents or Therapists Know About

By Isa Marrs, MA CCC-SLP

When a child is lacking Theory of Mind making and keeping friends is very difficult.

Theory of Mind is one of the main deficits in individuals on the Autistic Spectrum yet it is rarely known or understood by professionals who work with children with Autism. I know this because I ask them before they come to work with me. In order to work with a child with Autism you must understand what it means to not have Theory of Mind. Most often parents of children with Autism do not know what Theory of Mind is either.

Why It Is Important

It is important for them to know what this term means as it will give them a better understanding of why their children are having such difficulties. It also allows parents to predict situations that may be difficult for their children due to their absence of Theory of Mind. Even the highest functioning children with Autism most often do not have Theory of Mind.

Theory of Mind is the ability to not only understand that people have different beliefs, motivations, knowledge and moods but also understand how that affects their actions and behavior as well as our own.

Many experiments have been done over the years to demonstrate Theory of Mind. My favorite being the "Smarties test". In this experiment typically developing children, and children with Autism were shown a closed container with a Smarties label on it. They were then asked "What do you think is in here?" The children in both groups answered "Smarties".

They were then shown that the container contained pencils, not Smarties. Then they were asked a couple of other questions.

The first question being "When I first showed you this container, what did you think was in here?" The typically developing child answered "Smarties".

The children were then asked "When the next child comes in what will he think is inside here?" Again they responded with "Smarties".

When these two questions were asked to children with Autism the majority answered pencils to both questions.

What The Results Tell Us

The findings of this experiment revealed that most children with Autism do not have the ability to understand other people's different beliefs. Typically developing children will have this understanding at 3-4 years of age.

In a recent class of 5 children with one being on the Autistic Spectrum the deficit was clearly evident. I went around the table and asked each child what they would buy their parents, grandparents and even a baby for the holidays. The one little girl who was on the Autistic Spectrum answered a Barbie Doll for everyone.

It was clear that this was what she wanted for a holiday gift however she was unable to get inside anyone else's thoughts and decide what might be a good gift for them. You can see how these deficits will significantly impact social functioning in these children.

It is very important to note that lack of Theory of Mind is not a sign of intelligence. One can be of gifted intelligence and not have Theory of Mind.

What Can Be Done?

I am often asked if this deficit can be overcome and/or taught. The answer is both yes and no. With intervention some people with Autism will develop a basic level of Theory of Mind which helps them function better in the situation they are currently in. In other words we can teach skills that are situation dependent.

The good news is that when Theory of Mind is addressed early on the deficits can be less severe later in life.

What Should You Do?

If you have a child with an Autism Spectrum Disorder I invite you contact me today to find out how the Where I Can Be Me social skills program can help develop your child's Theory of Mind so he can have friends.

You may request a free information package now by calling me directly at 914.488.5282, or by calling my toll-free, hassle-free, 24hr recorded message information hotline 1.866.380.8340, or by visiting my special information request web-site: www.SocialSkillsWestchester.com

Isa Marrs is an internationally recognized speech language pathologist who has been helping children with ASD for over twenty years.

Figure 23.1: MARRS Advertising Example 1

Right Decision Guarantee
JOIN WITHOUT RISK

Join our program now and enjoy the benefits for over a month without risk. We call it our _"Right Decision Guarantee"_. That means you can take up until the start of your child's 5th week to decide if the Jumpstart Talking program is right for your child. If not, we'll refund your entire investment without hassle. We couldn't make you this offer if we weren't totally confident that our program is right for your child. You have absolutely nothing to lose by calling 914.488.5282 now.

Figure 23.2: MARRS Advertising Example 2

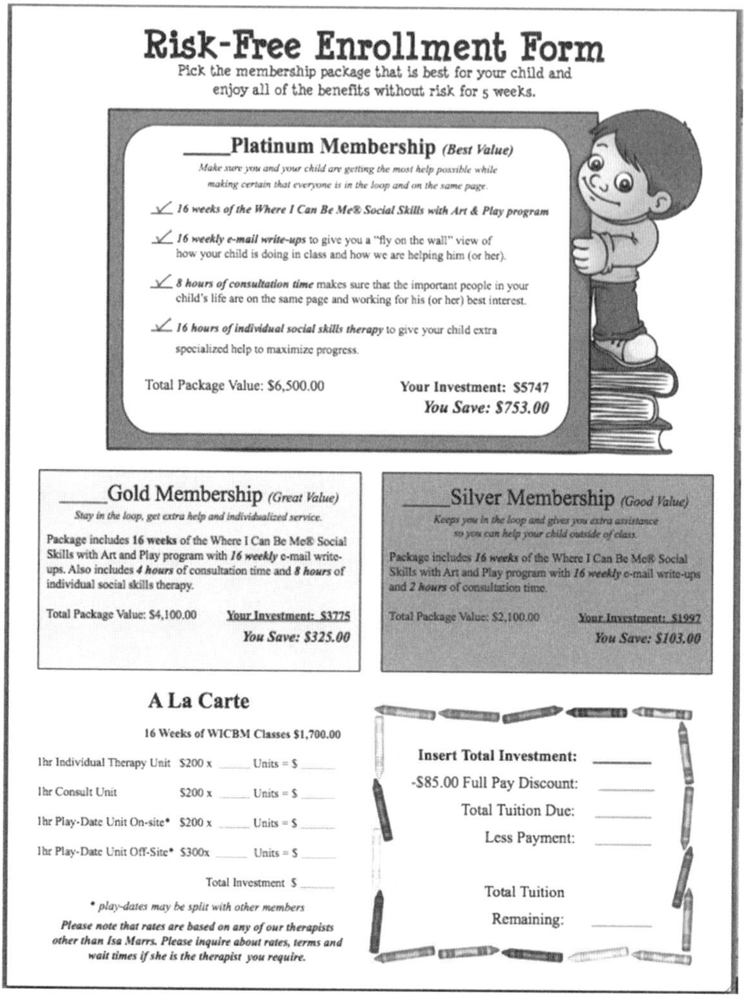

Risk-Free Enrollment Form

Pick the membership package that is best for your child and enjoy all of the benefits without risk for 5 weeks.

____Platinum Membership *(Best Value)*

Make sure you and your child are getting the most help possible while making certain that everyone is in the loop and on the same page.

✓ ***16 weeks of the Where I Can Be Me® Social Skills with Art & Play program***

✓ ***16 weekly e-mail write-ups*** to give you a "fly on the wall" view of how your child is doing in class and how we are helping him (or her).

✓ ***8 hours of consultation time*** makes sure that the important people in your child's life are on the same page and working for his (or her) best interest.

✓ ***16 hours of individual social skills therapy*** to give your child extra specialized help to maximize progress.

Total Package Value: $6,500.00 — **Your Investment: $5747** — ***You Save: $753.00***

____Gold Membership *(Great Value)*

Stay in the loop, get extra help and individualized service.

Package includes **16 weeks** of the Where I Can Be Me® Social Skills with Art and Play program with ***16 weekly*** e-mail write-ups. Also includes ***4 hours*** of consultation time and ***8 hours*** of individual social skills therapy.

Total Package Value: $4,100.00 — **Your Investment: $3775** — ***You Save: $325.00***

____Silver Membership *(Good Value)*

Keeps you in the loop and gives you extra assistance so you can help your child outside of class.

Package includes ***16 weeks*** of the Where I Can Be Me® Social Skills with Art and Play program with ***16 weekly*** e-mail write-ups and ***2 hours*** of consultation time.

Total Package Value: $2,100.00 — **Your Investment: $1997** — ***You Save: $103.00***

A La Carte

16 Weeks of WICBM Classes $1,700.00

1hr Individual Therapy Unit	$200 x	____ Units = $	____
1hr Consult Unit	$200 x	____ Units = $	____
1hr Play-Date Unit On-site*	$200 x	____ Units = $	____
1hr Play-Date Unit Off-Site*	$300x	____ Units = $	____
		Total Investment $	____

* *play-dates may be split with other members*

Please note that rates are based on any of our therapists other than Isa Marrs. Please inquire about rates, terms and wait times if she is the therapist you require.

Insert Total Investment: ____

-$85.00 Full Pay Discount: ____

Total Tuition Due: ____

Less Payment: ____

Total Tuition Remaining: ____

Figure 23.3: MARRS Advertising Example 3

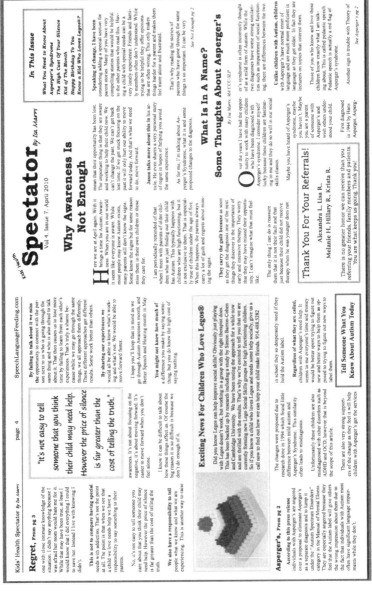

Figure 23.4: MARRS Advertising Example 4, Page 1

Figure 23.4: MARRS Advertising Example 4, Page 2

SECTION III

RESOURCES

An Offer from Jason Marrs
for readers of *No B.S. Price Strategy*

Dear Friend,

Hopefully, reading this book has convinced you: there's no better way to break free of "average" income and the sense of daily grind it produces than increasing your business' profits, and no better way to do that than by successfully increasing your prices. If you are ready for a thorough, in-depth, well-organized, foolproof SYSTEM for doing just that, then you'll be thrilled with my Simple Pricing System. It is the only pricing system developed for entrepreneurs by an entrepreneur (not by bean-counters). It goes beyond introducing and presenting different strategies as this book has done, to taking you step-by-step through the development of a pricing system custom built for your business. Essentially it is collaboration between you and I. Your use of this System is backed by a 365-day, complete satisfaction guarantee. To learn the details and discover how this System can give you more profit from the same effort, simply visit:

www.SimpleStrategicPricingSystem.com

While there, you can pick up a really cool bonus, just for stopping by! I'm not going to tell you what it is and take the surprise away. You'll have to go to the site to find out what it is. You can thank me later.

This is your opportunity to follow through on the interests that brought you this far, to and through this book, and actually engineer and implement improved price and profit strategy customized for your business.

Offer subject to change without notice.

Other Books by Dan Kennedy
Available at all booksellers
Information at www.NoBSBooks.com

No B.S. Series from Entrepreneur Press
No B.S. Wealth Attraction in The New Economy
No B.S. Business Success in The New Economy
No B.S. Sales Success in The New Economy
No B.S. Ruthless Management of People and Profits
No B.S. DIRECT Marketing for NON-Direct Marketing Businesses
No B.S. Marketing to the Affluent
No B.S. Time Management for Entrepreneurs

Ultimate Marketing Plan (Adams Media)
Ultimate Sales Letter (Adams Media)
Uncensored Sales Secrets—with Sydney Barrows (Entrepreneur Press)
New Psycho-Cybernetics—with Dr. Maxwell Maltz (Prentice Hall)
Making Them Believe—with Chip Kessler (Glazer-Kennedy Publishing)
Make 'Em Laugh & Take Their Money (Glazer-Kennedy Publishing)

Index